GLOBALVIEWPOINTS

Social Networking

D1265194

Other Books of Related Interest:

At Issue Series

Cyberbullying

Cyberpredators

Policing the Internet

Current Controversies Series

The Global Impact of Social Media

Politics and Media

Introducing Issues with Opposing Viewpoints Series

Cyberbullying

Media Bias

Opposing Viewpoints Series

Online Pornography

GLOBALVIEWPOINTS

Social Networking

Noah Berlatsky, Book Editor

GREENHAVEN PRESS
A part of Gale, Cengage Learning

GALE
CENGAGE Learning·

Detroit • New York • San Francisco • New Haven, Conn • Waterville, Maine • London

Elizabeth Des Chenes, *Director, Publishing Solutions*

© 2013 Greenhaven Press, a part of Gale, Cengage Learning

Gale and Greenhaven Press are registered trademarks used herein under license.

For more information, contact:
Greenhaven Press
27500 Drake Rd.
Farmington Hills, MI 48331-3535
Or you can visit our Internet site at gale.cengage.com

For product information and technology assistance, contact us at

Gale Customer Support, 1-800-877-4253
For permission to use material from this text or product, submit all requests online at
www.cengage.com/permissions

Further permissions questions can be emailed to permissionrequest@cengage.com

Articles in Greenhaven Press anthologies are often edited for length to meet page requirements. In addition, original titles of these works are changed to clearly present the main thesis and to explicitly indicate the author's opinion. Every effort is made to ensure that Greenhaven Press accurately reflects the original intent of the authors. Every effort has been made to trace the owners of copyrighted material.

Cover image © Samuel Aranda/Corbis.

LIBRARY OF CONGRESS CATALOGING-IN-PUBLICATION DATA

Social networking / Noah Berlatsky, book editor.
    p. cm. -- (Global viewpoints)
    Includes bibliographical references and index.
    ISBN 978-0-7377-6270-9 (hbk.) -- ISBN 978-0-7377-6446-8 (pbk.)
    1. Online social networks--Juvenile literature. 2. Social networks--Juvenile literature. I. Berlatsky, Noah.
    HM742.S6294 2013
    302.3--dc23
                                                    2012040006

Printed in the United States of America
1 2 3 4 5   17 16 15 14 13

Contents

The number of Facebook users in Britain, the United States, Norway, and other countries appears to be falling.

Chapter 2: Uses of Social Networking

Chapter 3: Social Networking and Democratic Movements

Social media does not necessarily promote democracy and peace. On the contrary, it can be used by authoritarian regimes to increase their power.

Chapter 4: Social Networking and Access to Information

Foreword

"The problems of all of humanity can only be solved by all of humanity."
—Swiss author Friedrich Dürrenmatt

Global interdependence has become an undeniable reality. Mass media and technology have increased worldwide access to information and created a society of global citizens. Understanding and navigating this global community is a challenge, requiring a high degree of information literacy and a new level of learning sophistication.

Building on the success of its flagship series, Opposing Viewpoints, Greenhaven Press has created the Global Viewpoints series to examine a broad range of current, often controversial topics of worldwide importance from a variety of international perspectives. Providing students and other readers with the information they need to explore global connections and think critically about worldwide implications, each Global Viewpoints volume offers a panoramic view of a topic of widespread significance.

Drugs, famine, immigration—a broad, international treatment is essential to do justice to social, environmental, health, and political issues such as these. Junior high, high school, and early college students, as well as general readers, can all use Global Viewpoints anthologies to discern the complexities relating to each issue. Readers will be able to examine unique national perspectives while, at the same time, appreciating the interconnectedness that global priorities bring to all nations and cultures.

Material in each volume is selected from a diverse range of sources, including journals, magazines, newspapers, nonfiction books, speeches, government documents, pamphlets, organization newsletters, and position papers. Global Viewpoints is truly global, with material drawn primarily from international sources available in English and secondarily from US sources with extensive international coverage.

Features of each volume in the Global Viewpoints series include:

- An **annotated table of contents** that provides a brief summary of each essay in the volume, including the name of the country or area covered in the essay.

- An **introduction** specific to the volume topic.

- A **world map** to help readers locate the countries or areas covered in the essays.

- For each viewpoint, an **introduction** that contains notes about the author and source of the viewpoint explains why material from the specific country is being presented, summarizes the main points of the viewpoint, and offers three **guided reading questions** to aid in understanding and comprehension.

- **For further discussion** questions that promote critical thinking by asking the reader to compare and contrast aspects of the viewpoints or draw conclusions about perspectives and arguments.

- A worldwide list of **organizations to contact** for readers seeking additional information.

- A **periodical bibliography** for each chapter and a **bibliography of books** on the volume topic to aid in further research.

- A comprehensive **subject index** to offer access to people, places, events, and subjects cited in the text, with the countries covered in the viewpoints highlighted.

Global Viewpoints is designed for a broad spectrum of readers who want to learn more about current events, history, political science, government, international relations, economics, environmental science, world cultures, and sociology— students doing research for class assignments or debates, teachers and faculty seeking to supplement course materials, and others wanting to understand current issues better. By presenting how people in various countries perceive the root causes, current consequences, and proposed solutions to worldwide challenges, Global Viewpoints volumes offer readers opportunities to enhance their global awareness and their knowledge of cultures worldwide.

Introduction

> *"The next billion people are coming on-line from India, China, and even Africa. . . . Massive numbers of people are going to come online from cultures we don't normally interact with."*
>
> —Jimmy Wales,
> cofounder of Wikipedia, quoted
> November 3, 2011, on BBC News

Wikipedia is a free, online encyclopedia written and edited by volunteer users. In other words, any individual can go online, find a Wikipedia article (for example, the article about social networking) and improve it by adding or deleting information. As of 2012 Wikipedia, which was founded in 2001, had more than twenty-two million articles in more than 280 languages, from Aceh to Žemaitėška. It is accessed by more than four hundred million users a month, and it is the fifth most popular website in the world.

Wikipedia is, first and foremost, an encyclopedia, where one can look up information on such topics as "Aceh" or "Žemaitėška." But it is also a social networking site, where individuals get together to work on a common project— creating an encyclopedia. Sarah Hartshorn in an August 25, 2010, post on Social Media Today explained that "Wikipedia is a social community and it takes content that users submit very seriously." Like any social community, Wikipedia has norms and rules, and new users must conform if they wish to participate. For example, Wikipedia's articles are supposed to be written from a neutral point of view. Articles that are written like opinion pieces or op-eds rather than like encyclopedia articles will generally be deleted or heavily edited by other users.

In part, because of its own social norms, Wikipedia has largely avoided connecting or partnering with other social media sites. Wikipedia does not include Facebook "Like" buttons or Google Plus links on its site. In comments made to Bianca Bosker in a November 26, 2011, article on the *Huffington Post*, Wikipedia cofounder Jimmy Wales gave several reasons for Wikipedia's lack of connection with other social media. In the first place, Wales said Wikipedia strives for neutrality, and so it tries to avoid favoring or endorsing other commercial websites such as Facebook. In addition, Wales said, privacy concerns about Facebook's data gathering have been an issue for the Wikipedia community. "If I go to read something on Wikipedia, that's my own personal business," Wales said. "You should feel safe and private knowing that whatever you want to learn, you go to Wikipedia to learn it and you don't have to worry that you've accidentally told Facebook you want to learn it."

Rather than partnering with other social media platforms, Wales believes Wikipedia should try to focus on reaching out to more users, particularly in the developing world. According to a January 2, 2012, article by Anna Heim on The Next Web, Wikipedia has a strong presence in English and Spanish, but there is significant "room for improvement" in other major languages, such as Mandarin, Arabic, and Portuguese. In the Yoruba language of Nigeria, there appears to be only one person doing major editing work, according to Wales, as quoted in a March 27, 2012, article by Jon Gambrell on the *Huffington Post*.

The Wikimedia Foundation (WMF), the nonprofit behind Wikipedia, is actively trying to improve Wikipedia's global presence. Heim reports that to draw in users from Portuguese-speaking Brazil, Wikipedia is planning to make its Portuguese-language instructions for editing clearer. It also hopes to encourage Brazilians to start using and editing the Portuguese-language articles rather than simply reading or translating

English ones. Currently, Heim reports, Wikipedia includes more than seven hundred thousand articles in Portuguese, but many are much shorter than their English counterparts. The WMF's chief global development officer Barry Newstead says that at the moment encouraging longer, more in-depth articles is more of a priority than simply expanding the number of articles available in the language.

Wikipedia has also tried to increase interest by borrowing ideas from other social networks. For instance, after a survey showing that editors contributed more when they felt valued, the site introduced a program called "WikiLove," according to an August 4, 2011, article by Leslie Horn at PCMag.com. WikiLove allows users to send messages of appreciation and icons to other Wikipedia editors. WMF is also trying to encourage professors to assign students to work on Wikipedia entries, particularly in India, Brazil, Canada, and Germany. These initiatives are especially important because Wikipedia is currently losing editors. Speaking to Horn, Wales said that the drop in editors might be in part because there are simply fewer topics uncovered and less work to do on the site. Wales said the loss of editors "is not a crisis," but he considers it to be important.

Wikipedia, then, relies on its users to generate content, tries to maintain its users' privacy, and is looking to expand its global reach while maintaining its hold on its early adopters. In the remainder of *Global Viewpoints: Social Networking*, these themes will surface repeatedly in chapters dealing with the popularity of social networking, uses of social networking, social networking and democratic movements, and social networking and access to information. Wikipedia is a unique website, but in many ways, its challenges and opportunities mirror those of social media as a whole.

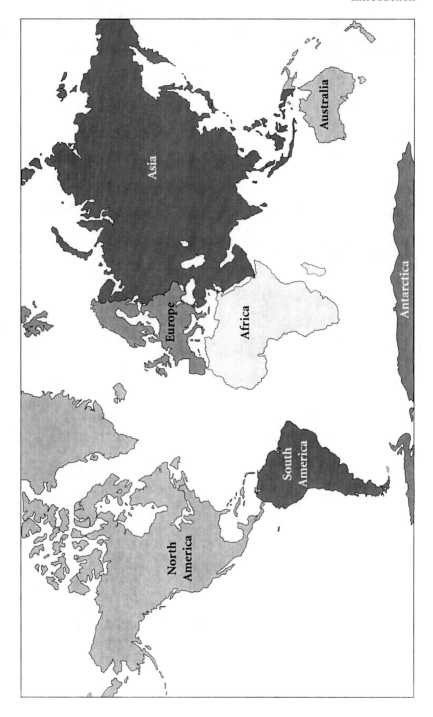

GLOBALVIEWPOINTS

The Popularity of Social Networking

The Philippines Leads the World in Social Networking

Jon Russell

Jon Russell is a Thailand-based social media consultant and Asia editor at global tech website The Next Web. In the following viewpoint, he reports that the Philippines is the top country for social networking in the world, with other Southeast Asian nations such as Indonesia and Malaysia close behind. He argues that this is because Asia got an early start on social networking. Facebook, he says, was able to capitalize on an already existing understanding and enthusiasm for social networking. Russell points out that many Asian countries were using social networking before the term "social networking" had even been invented.

As you read, consider the following questions:

1. What countries have the second, third, and fourth highest percentages of social network users, and what percentage of people in those countries use social networks?

2. According to Russell, why did social network users move to Facebook?

3. Which city does Russell say has the largest Facebook population, and how many users are there in that city?

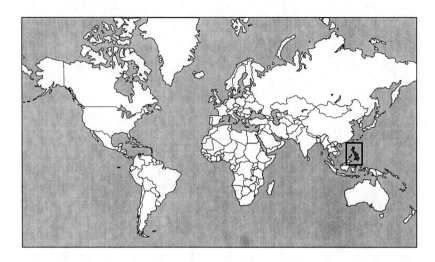

Asia dominates the world's biggest social networking mar-kets according to research from blog *24/7 Wall St.* who compiled a list of countries where Facebook penetration (usage per population) is highest.

The Philippines Tops the List

The Philippines tops the list with 93.9 percent of the nation reportedly signed up to Facebook, the full list is below with the summary from . . . [the Philippines] market following.

1. Philippines 93.9%

2. Israel 91%

3. Turkey 90.9%

4. Chile 90.2%

5. Argentina 89.2%

6. Malaysia 88.4%

7. Indonesia 87.5%

8. Peru 87.2%

9. Colombia 86.9%

10. Venezuela 86.2%

What is interesting is just how high Twitter usage . . . [is in the Philippines] while LinkedIn remains particularly low.

1. Philippines

> Facebook: 93.9%

> Twitter: 16.1%

> LinkedIn: 1.9%

> Internet Use: 29.7%

Social network penetration is incredibly high in the Philippines, reaching 95%. Facebook is the country's most popular website, more so than Google, and has a penetration rate of 93.9%. The Philippines is also the eighth most popular country for Twitter use on a global scale, with a penetration rate of 16.1%. The popularity of photo sharing has increased by 46% in the country in one year, largely due to Facebook. Social networking is so popular among Filipinos, the country has been nicknamed "The Social Networking Capital of the World."...

An Explanation

While the blog claims that "there is no obvious explanation" to explain why most of the 10 markets are developing, based in Latin America or Southeast Asian countries, I might hazard an explanation.

The country has been nicknamed "The Social Networking Capital of the World."

For Asia, and to a lesser extent Latin America, Facebook was able to tap into an existing understanding and usage of social networking, which helped bring in large user numbers over a relatively short time.

To explain, in many of these top 10 markets (and particularly in Asia) social networking . . . became popular, with ser-

Philippines Facebook Growth, 2008–2010

Users Dec. 31, 2008	Users Dec. 31, 2009	Users Dec. 31, 2010	12-month Growth	24-month Growth
390,700	8,387,560	18,901,900	125.4%	4,738%

TAKEN FROM: Nick Burcher, "Facebook Usage Statistics Dec 31st 2010 vs Dec 31st 2009 vs Dec 31st 2008," *Nick Burcher*, January 4, 2011. www.nickburcher.com.

vices like Friendster and Hi5 the first to garner a sizeable audience at the same time that Facebook was beginning its early growth in the US, UK and other Western markets.

Once Facebook's word-of-mouth got beyond these Western areas and into Asia around 2008/2009, social networkers were already well established (as a genre), meaning that users began abandoning Friendster, Hi5 and others they had been using in favour of Facebook; large numbers of already established peer networks moved over [to] them, building huge momentum and awareness in their markets.

For Asia, and to a lesser extent Latin America, Facebook was able to tap into an existing understanding and usage of social networking.

Equally, [social network] users were moving to Facebook because it was better—games, features, etc.—and not just because they were trying it out, so users in Asia were generally more loyal, motivated and spent more time using it.

Compare that to the US and UK where Facebook was the first, well-known social network to emerge. It was tasked with not only promoting its product, but establishing social networking as a popular habit in the first place.

The argument may also justify why Twitter and LinkedIn have far less market share in these countries as both services are the front-runners for microblogging and business social networking (respectively), and thus do not tap into a 'ready made market'; though clearly neither has the mass market appeal of Facebook, which is a major explanation for their lower usage.

As a market, Asia is particularly well known for online sites and sharing with forums and other types of services long popular in many countries, before the term social network had ever been coined.

I've not had the opportunity to check through the figures yet but the Philippines is often heralded as the Facebook capital of the world, while Indonesia and Malaysia are equally as well known for strong social media usage.

UPDATE: . . . Although the Philippines has the highest proportion of users per population, Indonesia's capital, Jakarta, has the largest Facebook population of any city in the world (17.5 million users).

Indonesian Society Is Enamored with Social Networking

Sarah Mishkin

Sarah Mishkin is a journalist for the Financial Times. *In the following viewpoint, she reports that there is massive and growing use of social media in Indonesia. She says this is in part because Indonesian culture is chatty and social, and also because Indonesian online use was low until relatively recently. Thus, she says, Indonesians stalled using social media when they started using the Internet and now are more comfortable with it than many Western Internet users. Mishkin says many Indonesians do not have access to credit cards for digital payments, so companies have had to innovate in billing practices. She notes that Indonesia has become a place for international companies to experiment with social media marketing.*

As you read, consider the following questions:

1. What is *Republik Twitter*, according to the viewpoint?

2. According to Mishkin, what are the most popular ways for Indonesian Internet users to get online?

3. Who is Maicih, and what is his social network marketing strategy, according to Mishkin?

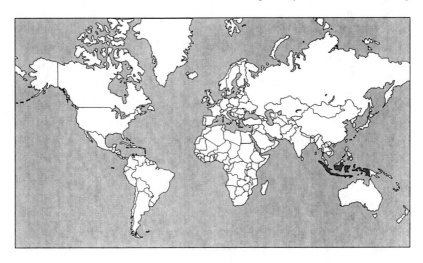

More than 600m people around the world have down-loaded the hit mobile phone game Angry Birds over the past two years. But when Rovio, the game's Finland-based developer, unveiled an Angry Birds Facebook app [application] last month [February 2012], its executives decided to hold the global launch event in Jakarta.

A Love Affair with Social Media

In the same week, cinemagoers in the city were treated to the release of *Republik Twitter*, an Indonesian romantic drama about a young man who manages a politician's Twitter account while falling in love with a journalist whose tweets he follows. Like Rovio's executives, the film's producers recognise that the bigger love affair going on is that between Indonesians and social media.

Even though fewer than 25 per cent of Indonesia's 240m citizens are online, the country is already Facebook's third-largest market, with 43m users, according to Socialbakers, a web analytics agency. Meanwhile, the country is Twitter's fifth-largest market in terms of market penetration, with 27 per cent of its web users tweeting, according to ComScore, the market research company.

These dynamics have made Indonesia a test case for companies looking for growth in booming emerging markets, where people are logging on to the Internet but developing different online habits to those of consumers in the West. While users in London or New York typically access the Internet through laptops and use credit or debit cards to make online purchases, users in Jakarta are more likely to pick up their BlackBerry or, increasingly, their cheap smartphone, go straight to their favourite social network, and make any purchases via money transfer or cash.

The bigger love affair going on is that between Indonesians and social media.

"In a traditional world, you would say if people have lots of money and credit cards, then the online space works," says Nirvik Singh, ad agency Grey Group's chairman for Asia Pacific. But in Indonesia, he says, "flip that around".

One reason social media has taken such a hold is because the local culture is naturally social and chatty. BlackBerry's messaging service, which lets users chat among themselves for free, has for years helped it dominate the local market.

Added to that has been rapid mobile Internet growth. Indonesia has achieved what Steven Goh, founder of Mig33, a social network popular in the country, describes as a "massive trifecta": the spread of data-enabled phones, fast telecom [telecommunications] networks, and cheap data plans, some of which offer special rates for users who want to use their phones mostly for accessing Facebook and Twitter.

Access Through Phones

Just 7 per cent of Indonesians had a PC [personal computer] in 2011, but 90 per cent have access to a mobile phone, says Vaishali Rastogi, a partner and managing director at Boston Consulting Group in Singapore. "Mobile connectivity is getting ubiquitous," she adds. "For many it's about first-time access, and for others it is convenience."

Some Indonesians without computers still use Internet cafés, known locally as *warnets*, but increasingly they are getting online through Android-powered smartphones or less powerful, cheaper handsets known as feature phones that often come pre-programmed with social networking applications.

James Fergusson, head of technology at market research company TNS, notes that about a third of Indonesians who use the Internet did so for the first time in the past two years. "This means that the people who are online in Indonesia have jumped straight into Web 2.0. They never experienced Internet 1.0, when the Internet was only one way," he says. "The main portal into the Internet, particularly in a market like Indonesia, is often the social network."

---

*Just 7 per cent of Indonesians had a [personal computer]
in 2011, but 90 per cent have access to a mobile phone.*

As a result, consumers in emerging markets are far less hostile than US and European consumers to brands that use social networks for marketing, according to TNS research.

This provides an opportunity for Western companies that might be wary of having too heavy-handed a social media presence in their home markets. Grey Group's Mr Singh says interest among aspirational local consumers in brands such as Starbucks and Oakley have made their Facebook pages some of the most popular in the country. Nokia, for instance, created a Facebook game as part of a marketing campaign in 2009 that allowed users to input data about their Internet activities and compete to see who was the most social. The campaign, led by an affiliate of Young & Rubicam, was so successful that the company then used the idea in other markets.

Indonesia, Asia, and Social Media

While some areas, such as China and India, have Internet penetration rates below 25 per cent, others, like Hong Kong, South Korea, Japan, Australia and Singapore, boast numbers rivalling anywhere in the world.

Certain Southeast Asian markets, like Singapore, Indonesia and Malaysia, have Facebook dominating the social networking space. In Vietnam, however—as in Mainland China—Facebook has been blocked by the government.... Indonesia is one of Twitter's biggest markets in terms of user penetration, and Jakarta, Indonesia's capital city, boasts 1 per cent of the world's tweets daily—giving it the dubious title of "the world's Twitter capital."

India, paradoxically, is one of Asia's largest social media markets in terms of sheer size and potential but is one of the smallest in terms of Internet penetration. India's potential has yet to be tapped—her growing, massive middle class of over 300 million people makes it a market to watch out for, as infrastructure develops and users connect with each other and brands and products online.

Christer Holloman, The Social Media MBA: Your Competitive Edge in Social Media Strategy Development & Delivery. *West Sussex, UK: John Wiley & Sons, 2012, p. 216.*

For Rovio, launching the Angry Birds Facebook app will help them access those users whose phones are capable of accessing the web but are not sophisticated enough to download a stand-alone application, says Henri Holm, Rovio's senior vice president for Asia.

Innovations in Billing

The company is considering pitches from local payment providers who can help it take the next step: to monetise its Indonesian business despite the country's relatively unsophisticated payment systems, allowing users to buy extras. "In Indonesia you have to count on micropayments, you have to count on mobile devices, you have to work on billing integration," says Mr Holm. "We need to have a very localised way of operating—you need to be extremely innovative."

Local and regional start-ups are overcoming the credit-card gap with strategies that range from the complex to the simple, like the one used by Maicih, a maker of flavoured cassava crisps, a traditional snack. Founded by 24-year-old Reza Nurhilman nearly two years ago, the company sells the snack at roving stands whose changing locations are broadcast continuously to Maicih's nearly 400,000 Twitter followers.

[The] local media culture . . . gives an advantage to social media–focused campaigns and businesses over traditional online stores.

Whereas in the West this business model might simply be an adjunct to wider marketing efforts, it forms the basis of Maicih's strategy. Mr Nurhilman says the idea came when friends began writing testimonies on Facebook and Twitter. "Then I thought, why not use Facebook and Twitter for marketing Maicih, because everyone is on [them], it is free, easy, and the network is unlimited?"

Maicih now has its own factory in Bandung, about 1,500 vendors throughout the country, and plans eventually to open a café.

Maicih's success illustrates what Elwin Mok, managing creative director at Celsius, a Jakarta-based ad agency, describes as a local Internet culture that gives an advantage to social media–focused campaigns and businesses over traditional online stores. "Indonesia is not really search-savvy, not really accustomed to using Google to search for things," he says. So for companies looking to get their products noticed online, he says, "it's very important that they can . . . make it a conversation".

Africa Is Beginning to Experience a Boom in Social Networking Using Mobile Phones

André-Michel Essoungou

André-Michel Essoungou is a writer for Africa Renewal, *a United Nations magazine based in New York City. In the following viewpoint, he reports that Africa is experiencing rapid growth in social media usage. He says that this growth is related to more and more people accessing social media through mobile phones. Essoungou says that Africa's Internet usage is low, but that mobile phones are helping people without land access to connect online. He concludes that the growing number of Internet and social media users, and the resultant business opportunities, are attracting media companies to and local innovation within the African market.*

As you read, consider the following questions:

1. As noted in the viewpoint, what is the most visited website in Africa, and how has it grown over the past few years?

2. According to Essoungou, what is the rate of Internet use in Africa, and how does this compare to Internet use worldwide?

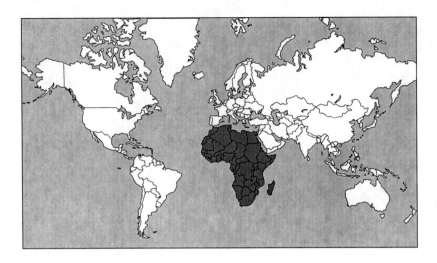

3. What is Baraza, and what will it allow online users to do, according to Essoungou?

In the mid-1990s, as the use of mobile phones started its rapid spread in much of the developed world, few thought of Africa as a potential market. Now, with more than 400 million subscribers, its market is larger than North America's. Africa took the lead in the global shift from fixed to mobile telephones, notes a report by the UN [United Nations] International Telecommunication Union. Rarely has anyone adopted mobile phones faster and with greater innovation.

Mobile Internet Use

A similar story now seems again to be unfolding. Africans are coupling their already extensive use of cell phones with a more recent and massive interest in social media—Internet-based tools and platforms that allow people to interact with each other much more than in the past. In the process, Africans are leading what may be the next global trend: a major shift to mobile Internet use, with social media as its main drivers. According to Mary Meeker, an influential Internet analyst, mobile Internet and social media are the fastest-growing areas of the technology industry worldwide, and she predicts that mobile Internet use will soon overtake fixed Internet use.

Studies suggest that when Africans go online (predominantly with their mobile phones) they spend much of their time on social media platforms (Facebook, Twitter, YouTube and so on). Sending and reading e-mails, reading news and posting research queries have become less important activities for Africans.

In recent months Facebook—the major social media platform worldwide and currently the most visited website in most of Africa—has seen massive growth on the continent. The number of African Facebook users now stands at over 17 million, up from 10 million in 2009. More than 15 per cent of people online in Africa are currently using the platform, compared to 11 per cent in Asia. Two other social networking websites, Twitter and YouTube, rank among the most visited websites in most African countries.

Africans are leading what may be the next global trend: a major shift to mobile Internet use, with social media as its main drivers.

Along with regular citizens, African stars, thinkers, political leaders and companies have rapidly joined the global conversation. The Facebook fan base of Côte d'Ivoire's football star and UN goodwill ambassador Didier Drogba is more than 1 million people. Zambian best-selling author and economist Dambisa Moyo has more than 26,000 followers on Twitter. Media organizations in South Africa and companies such as Kenya Airways are using various social media platforms to interact better with customers and readers. During recent elections in Côte d'Ivoire candidates did not only tour cities and villages; they also moved the contest online, feverishly posting campaign updates on Twitter and Facebook.

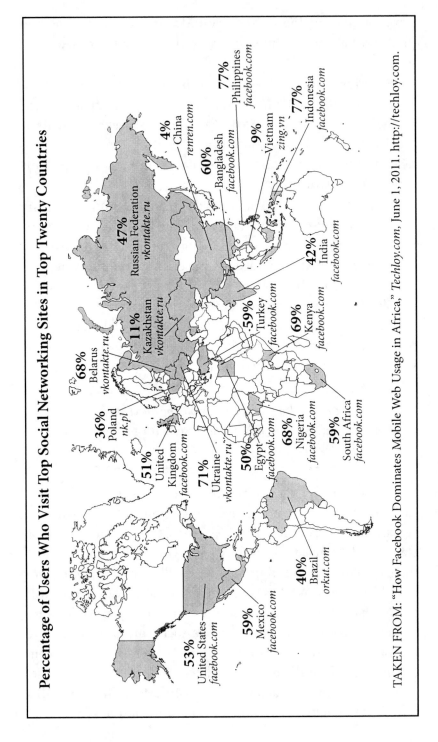

Percentage of Users Who Visit Top Social Networking Sites in Top Twenty Countries

68%
Belarus
vkontakte.ru

36%
Poland
nk.pl

51%
United
Kingdom
facebook.com

71%
Ukraine
vkontakte.ru

50%
Egypt
facebook.com

47%
Russian Federation
vkontakte.ru

11%
Kazakhstan
vkontakte.ru

4%
China
renren.com

60%
Bangladesh
facebook.com

77%
Philippines
facebook.com

9%
Vietnam
zing.vn

77%
Indonesia
facebook.com

42%
India
facebook.com

59%
Turkey
facebook.com

69%
Kenya
facebook.com

68%
Nigeria
facebook.com

59%
South Africa
facebook.com

53%
United States
facebook.com

59%
Mexico
facebook.com

40%
Brazil
orkut.com

TAKEN FROM: "How Facebook Dominates Mobile Web Usage in Africa," *Techloy.com*, June 1, 2011. http://techloy.com.

Constraints and Opportunities

Africa's upward trend in the use of social media is even more striking given the low number of Africans connected to the Internet and the many hurdles Africans face in trying to go online.

"The widespread availability of mobile phones means that the mobile web can reach tens of millions more than the wired web."

Africa's Internet users (more than 100 million at the end of 2010) represent just a small percentage of the 2 billion people online around the world. In the US alone, more than 220 million people use the Internet. Within Africa, one person out of every 10 is estimated to be an Internet user (up from one in 5,000 back in 1998), making the continent the region in the world with the lowest penetration rate.

Among the many reasons for this poor showing are the scarcity and prohibitive costs of broadband connections (the fastest means of accessing the Internet) and the limited number of personal computers in use.

But these challenges simultaneously contribute to Africa's impressive growth rate in the use of mobile Internet, which in recent years has been the highest in the world. "Triple-digit growth rates are routine across the continent," notes Jon [Stephenson] von Tetzchner, cofounder of Opera [Software ASA], the world's most popular Internet browser for mobile phones. "The widespread availability of mobile phones means that the mobile web can reach tens of millions more than the wired web." Mr. Tetzchner believes that like mobile phones, whose use has grown rapidly in Africa in recent years, the "mobile web is beginning to reshape the economic, political and social development of the continent."

"Seismic Shift" Coming

Erik Hersman, a prominent African social media blogger and entrepreneur who helped drive development of the ground-breaking platform Ushahidi, is equally enthusiastic. In an e-mail to *Africa Renewal*, he notes that "with mobile phone penetration already high across the continent, and as we get to critical mass with Internet usage in some of Africa's leading countries (Kenya, South Africa, Ghana, Nigeria, Egypt) . . . a seismic shift will happen with services, products and information."

The sense that the future holds more promise is inducing major companies to show special interest in Africa's expanding pool of Internet users. Facebook, after launching versions in some of the major African languages (including Swahili, Hausa and Zulu) in May [2010], has announced it will offer free access to its platform to mobile phone users in various countries around the world, including many in Africa. In October Google started testing a new service for Swahili speakers in east and central Africa. Tentatively called Baraza ("meeting place" in Swahili), it will allow people to interact and share knowledge by asking and answering questions, many of them of only very local or regional interest.

The sense that the future holds more promise is inducing major companies to show special interest in Africa's expanding pool of Internet users.

Africans are also getting ready to benefit from the fast-growing mobile Internet sector. In South Africa, Mxit, a free instant messaging application with an estimated 7 million users, is the most popular local social networking platform. From Abidjan [in the Côte d'Ivoire] and Accra [in Ghana] to Lusaka [in Zambia] and Nairobi [in Kenya], African programmers are designing, testing and launching new homegrown platforms and tools to keep the African online conversation going.

The Japanese Tsunami May Spur More Widespread Use of Social Media

Eric Johnston

Eric Johnston is a staff writer for the Japan Times. *In the following viewpoint, he says that the March 2011 disaster in Japan—in which an earthquake and tsunami caused great damage, including serious failures at many nuclear power plants—raised the profile of social media. Johnston says that a significant number of Japanese citizens used social media sites like Twitter, Facebook, and YouTube to find information about the disaster. In some cases, he says, social media seemed to provide more trustworthy information than official sources. On the other hand, he says, hoaxes and scams on social media sites raised public and government concerns.*

As you read, consider the following questions:

1. According to Johnston, in what way did the 1995 Great Hanshin Earthquake affect Japan's use of cell phones?
2. What did Mayor Katsunobu Sakurai post on YouTube, and what effect did it have, according to Johnston?
3. According to the Nomura Research Institute's survey, from what sources (and in what percentages) did Japanese find information about the disaster?

Eric Johnston, "Will 3/11 Prove Social Media Watershed?," *The Japan Times*, March 8, 2012. Copyright © 2012 by The Japan Times. All rights reserved. Reproduced by permission.

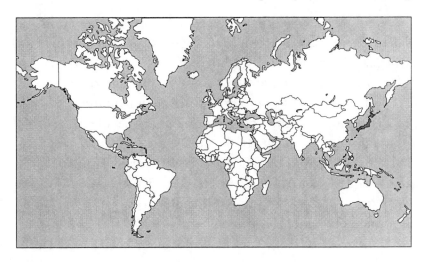

Massive disasters that claim thousands of lives and change communities forever sometimes also spur the development of radical new technologies, or new ways of applying existing techniques, that otherwise may have occurred more slowly, if at all.

Twitter and the Tsunami

Prior to the 1995 Great Hanshin Earthquake, for example, cell phones were gaining in popularity but were far from ubiquitous. Until the 7.3-magnitude temblor shattered Kobe and its vicinity, they had competed with personal handy-phone systems (PHS), which were less expensive but also less reliable and of limited reception. In the Kobe disaster, it became apparent PHS technology wasn't nearly advanced enough to quickly track down loved ones in an emergency. A year or so later, cell phones were everywhere and PHS phones were becoming obsolete.

In future years, last March's [2011] megaquake and tsunami, along with the nuclear disaster they triggered [as power plants were destabilized], may come to be viewed as a similar watershed moment for social media.

Admittedly, it had become clear well before the Great East Japan Earthquake that while the Mixi social networking site, which is domestic only, was huge, Twitter's popularity had exploded in Japan and Facebook's star was on the rise.

But the triple disaster created new opportunities for social media, allowing unprecedented numbers of people to exchange vast amounts of information in real time.

The role played by social media was particularly crucial in the first few hours and days after the 9.0-magnitude quake deep below the Pacific seabed generated a tsunami that would devastate the Tohoku region's coast.

Twitter, Facebook, YouTube and other social media provided a window for survivors to alert and keep the outside world informed about what was happening in the disaster areas, search for their loved ones, and provide updates and analysis of statements released by the government and Tokyo Electric Power Co. [Tepco] on the unfolding Fukushima [Daiichi] No. 1 nuclear plant disaster.

The triple disaster created new opportunities for social media, allowing unprecedented numbers of people to exchange vast amounts of information in real time.

Famously, Minamisoma mayor Katsunobu Sakurai, part of whose city falls inside the 20-km [kilometer] no-go zone around the leaking nuclear plant, went on YouTube about two weeks after March 11 to vent his anger at the central government's lack of response and to plead for international aid.

The video he posted garnered 200,000 hits, and resulted in truckloads of supplies being shipped to Minamisoma from other parts of the country and even overseas, generated extensive international media coverage of the city's plight, and prompted apologetic phone calls from the chief cabinet secretary and from Tepco.

Many Relied on Social Media

According to a survey of about 3,200 people by Nomura Research Institute late last March on the domestic media's response in the immediate aftermath of 3/11, TV coverage ranked extremely high as a source of vital disaster-related information, followed by portal sites, social media sites and newspaper sites.

In the multiple-answer survey, some 80.5 percent of respondents said [Japan's public broadcasting organization] NHK's broadcasts were a crucial source of information, while 56.9 percent said they relied on information from private TV broadcasters. This was followed by 43.2 percent who said they depended on portals such as Yahoo and Google, in addition to the home pages of newspapers and broadcasters.

Twitter, Facebook, YouTube and other social media provided a window for survivors to alert and keep the outside world informed about what was happening in the disaster areas.

Some 36 percent relied on conventional newspapers, another 18.6 percent said the websites of newspapers served as their primary source of information, while 18.3 percent of respondents said they relied on social media, including Twitter, Mixi and Facebook.

The Nomura survey also asked about the trustworthiness of information, but in this area, the picture is a bit more complex.

The poll found 28.8 percent of respondents had more trust in NHK after March 11, 17.5 percent had more faith in Yahoo and Google, and 13.4 percent had more trust in information from individual social media sites.

On the other hand, 28.9 percent of pollees said their distrust of information from the central and local governments had increased, 13.7 percent expressed rising doubts about

Social Media in Japan

High-tech social media have played a significant role in reducing the inward-looking stance of the Japanese and contributing to a global outlook in their mind-set and behavior.

Facebook got off to a slow start when it was inaugurated in Japan in 2008 because of competing Japanese social sites like Mixi, but things changed in 2010 when students and graduates of Japan's most prestigious universities began using the American site to search for jobs, resulting in several million users jumping onto the Facebook bandwagon. . . .

Facebook became even hotter as a result of its amazing role during and following the great earthquake and tsunami that struck the Fukushima area northeast of Tokyo in the spring of 2011. The dramatic online images of the tsunami as it was coming in and then the devastation it caused made Facebook a household name.

The new users of Facebook were not put off by the fact that using the site required them to use their real names—something Japanese sites did not do and something the Japanese had previously been reluctant to do. That was a relatively minor but still significant change in Japanese culture, and Facebook has continued to play an important role in the Japanese becoming less ethnocentric and more open to the outside world.

However, despite these domestic and international factors and the ongoing changes in many of Japan's larger corporations, traditional attitudes and practices remain significant elements in their business etiquette and ethics.

Boyé Lafayette De Mente,
Japan: Understanding & Dealing with
the New Japanese Way of Doing Business!
San Francisco, CA: Phoenix Books, 2012.

commercial TV as a reliable source and 9 percent said they had less faith in social media.

"The reason for the decline in trust in social media was that while many respondents said it was a very convenient source of disaster-related information, they also felt it provided increased opportunities for disseminating false or exaggerated information," the survey said.

Ayumi Fukaya, a Tokyo-based social media consultant, surveyed the tweets people were sending in the immediate aftermath of March 11 and analyzed them against a database of 80,000 words, dividing them into "positive" and "negative" sentiments.

One trend she noticed was that after then chief cabinet secretary Yukio Edano spoke on TV, people's positive tweets rose as his words appeared to calm them.

Yet social media's ability to rapidly reach large numbers of people also raised difficult ethical and legal questions after March 11 and about the effects of unverified reports on society, such as intentionally misleading information and especially moneymaking scams and hoaxes.

Fighting Hoaxes

Fukaya said hoaxes and false information were a problem immediately after March 11 on Twitter, but her analysis showed that tweets returned to more stable patterns within days.

"There were lots of examples of hoaxes on social media, such as reports of black rain [nuclear fallout] in Chiba Prefecture," Fukaya said. "But what I noticed after March 13 was the ratio of positive and negative tweets returned to normal patterns."

The various rumors and hoaxes that flourished on social media in the days and weeks after the quake were tracked by others attempting to prove or debunk some of those that were especially prevalent.

For example, chain e-mails with photo attachments purportedly showing masses of bodies washed up on the shores of Fukushima Prefecture were later identified as images of Asian victims of the 2004 Indian Ocean tsunami.

Another hoax that came to light was a series of fake e-mails, supposedly sent by the Japan Medical Association, warning people to avoid going outdoors if it rained because of the alleged danger from radiation. Yet other chain e-mails claimed people could avoid radiation poisoning by eating "wakame" seaweed.

Internet hoaxes . . . alarmed the central government and forced it to look for ways to monitor false data disseminated via the Internet or social media.

Toru Saito, a social media expert and CEO [chief executive officer] of Loops Communications Inc., said in a report on social media trends after the quake that media that make it hard to send anonymous posts would likely gain more currency.

"There was a rapid spread on Twitter and 2channel (Japan's largest Internet bulletin board) of information that was anonymous, open and virtual," Saito said of 3/11's immediate aftermath. But he added that he believes users will be more inclined in the future to prefer closed sites. "To ensure the trustworthiness of information, people are likely to be more interested in (using) a closed social media world with the person's real name," he said.

Internet hoaxes, the spread of false information, especially about radioactive fallout and scams such as calls for donations to bogus charities, alarmed the central government and forced it to look for ways to monitor false data disseminated via the Internet or social media.

Some of the steps taken, however, sparked censorship worries.

A report in May by the Telecom Services Association revealed instances where authorities had requested that information be deleted from a community website, in one case on grounds that it constituted false claims about the manufacturers of the Fukushima [Daiichi] reactors.

The association, which is made up of a broad range of telecom firms, including Internet service providers, also complied with another government request to remove photos of dead bodies from a blog. It also agreed to remove a blog posting the addresses of Tepco executives.

Those requests raised fears about looming state censorship. Most social media experts, however, say that given the present realities, that's not very likely.

"Social media in Japan are too diverse, while the technology itself continues to evolve rapidly. I don't think government censorship is possible," said Fukaya, the social media consultant.

Facebook's Popularity May Have Peaked in the United Kingdom and Other Western Nations

Charles Arthur

Charles Arthur is the technology editor for the Guardian. *In the following viewpoint, he reports that the number of Facebook users is falling in countries such as the United States, Canada, and Britain, where it has been established for years. Though Facebook continues to grow rapidly in places like Brazil and Mexico, its overall growth rate may be slowing. Arthur says that the fall in users in the West may hinder the chance of Facebook reaching its goal of one billion users worldwide. Facebook is also hampered by the fact that it has been banned in China, Arthur says.*

As you read, consider the following questions:

1. According to Arthur, when does Facebook use in any country seem to peak?

2. What specific Facebook initiative does Arthur say recently drew criticism?

3. When did Facebook first launch to the public, and what group did it cater to before that?

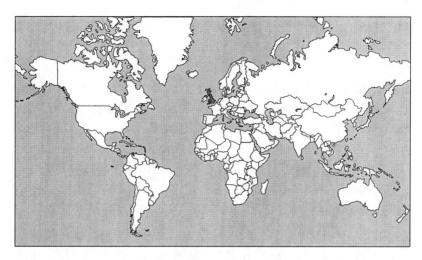

The number of people using Facebook has dropped in the UK [United Kingdom] for the second month in a row [in June 2011], mirroring similar falls in the US [United States], Canada and Norway, giving the first signs that the social network's popularity may be waning in the West.

Will Facebook Reach 1 Billion?

The website continued to grow worldwide, hitting an all-time high of 687 million users, according to data from the tracking company Inside Facebook, which uses Facebook's own advertising tools to determine the number of people using the site every month. Growth slowed however, having risen by 13.9m accounts in April and then just 11.8m in May. Typically in the past year it has grown by 20m a month. That slowdown could thwart founder Mark Zuckerberg's ambition to reach 1 billion users worldwide, despite his prediction last June that "it is almost a guarantee that it will happen". [Editor's note: Facebook reached one billion users in September 2012.]

Growth in Facebook use seems to peak in any country once the site is used by roughly half of those who have Internet connections—though with more than 2 billion people online worldwide, the site could still reach the 1 billion figure.

However, it would need people who have joined the site to stay with it—and that hasn't been happening in some countries.

Magnus Hoglund, chief executive of the law media portal Law360.com, who has worked on digital media companies for the past decade, said: "From my experience, I get the sense that being on Facebook is not cool anymore. The early adopters and trendsetters are moving away. [But] these are also exactly the type of people brand advertisers want to reach; if they are leaving, it doesn't look good for Facebook."

The site has been criticised in the West for its approach to users' privacy, with repeated protests about the way in which controls on data access are relaxed. Last week the revelation that it had extended an automatic facial recognition system for tagging photos beyond the US without asking people if they wanted to opt in drew criticism from privacy groups and security consultants.

A spokeswoman for Facebook said: "We are very pleased with our growth and with the way people are engaged with Facebook. More than 50% of our active users log on to Facebook in any given day."

"I get the sense that being on Facebook is not cool anymore."

The drop in use was most marked in the US, where numbers fell from May's 155.2 million, just under half the 239m people online, to 149.4 million at the start of June. It marked the first time in a year that the number of people logging in to the site over a month had fallen. In the UK, the fall was smaller at around 100,000 users to 29.8 million, or 58% of the 51.4 million people online. Canada saw a fall of 1.62 million to 16.6 million, while Norway also saw a fall of around 100,000 users over the month.

The fastest-growing countries, including Brazil and Mexico, grew at a maximum of 10% over the month.

Banned in China

The fall in users is most marked in those developed countries where Facebook first launched to the public in September 2006, after its first two years when it catered only to US college and high school users.

Eric Eldon, one of the researchers at Inside Facebook, said that it was hard to see how the social networking site could hit its 1 billion target except by getting into China, which has 420 million Internet users but just 391,000 Facebook users as of March. The site has been banned in China since 2008, while cloned versions abound inside the country. Zuckerberg visited China in December 2010, which led to speculation that he was working on a way to get the site approved by the government, but there has been no further detail on whether that is happening.

Facebook still dominates the world in terms of social network use, with Russia and China marking the biggest holdouts where homegrown networks are the most popular.

Hoglund added that following the stock market flotation of LinkedIn, Yandex and Groupon's plans to go public, this summer could mark the high-water mark for media and technology market offerings as firms rush to cash in before their capital runs out.

Meanwhile, reports in the US suggest that Facebook may have to make a public share offering at the beginning of 2012 because it will have more than 500 shareholders. US Securities and Exchange Commission rules oblige companies to make a listing once they've passed this threshold. Facebook did not respond to the *Guardian* on the issue.

[Editor's note: Facebook held its initial public offering May 18, 2012.]

Periodical and Internet Sources Bibliography

The following articles have been selected to supplement the diverse views presented in this chapter.

Biz Community (Cape Town, South Africa)	"Africa: Social Media Marketing in Continent," April 18, 2012.
Economist	"Social Media in Indonesia: Eat, Pray, Tweet," January 6, 2011.
Apostolis Fotiadis	"Greece: Social Media Advances Against Elite Owners," Inter Press Service, September 16, 2011. www.ipsnews.net.
Zoe Fox	"Facebook Finally Beats Google's Orkut . . . in Brazil," Mashable, January 17, 2012. http://mashable.com.
Shinichiro Kinjo	"How the 'Shy' Japanese Are Using Social Media," *Freshtrax*, December 26, 2012. http://blog.btrax.com.
Trevor Neethling	"Scramble Is On for Social Media Users in Africa," *BusinessDay*, March 20, 2012.
Nadia Samie	"Social Media Popular with South African Youth," Voice of America, October 18, 2011. www.voanews.com.
Paul Sawers	"Why Twitter Outguns Facebook in Japan," The Next Web, February 2, 2011. http://thenextweb.com.
Jan Vermeulen	"Biggest Social Networks in South Africa," MyBroadband, February 24, 2012. http://mybroadband.co.za.
Ingeborg Volan	"Twitter Launches Danish, Finnish, Norwegian Version," Social Media Nordic, December 21, 2011. http://socialmedianordic.com.

GLOBALVIEWPOINTS

CHAPTER 2

Uses of
Social Networking

In Western Europe, Journalists Make Increasing Use of Social Networks in Their Reporting

Cision

Cision is an international company that develops software for corporate communications and public relations. In the following viewpoint, the company reports on a survey that shows that journalists in the United Kingdom, France, and Germany are using social media more often in their work. The survey suggests that journalists use social media to gather information as well as promote their own work and writing. The survey shows that journalists believe that public relations professionals could do a better job using social media. Cision says that journalists still use traditional forms of research and reporting; social media has supplemented rather than replaced other forms of information gathering.

As you read, consider the following questions:

1. What does Cision say have been the consequences of Web 2.0 technologies for news organizations?

2. In the United Kingdom, which networking sites were identified as the most important social technology for journalism, according to the Cision survey?

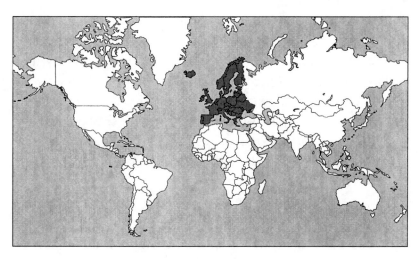

3. According to the survey, how do public relations professional mostly communicate with journalists?

A broad online survey across all media was conducted by
Cision, in conjunction with the University of Sunderland.
The survey included journalists from the UK [United King-
dom], France and Germany, and is designed to enhance the
media industry's understanding of social media uptake and
the impact of social media technologies and processes on
journalists' work. A total of 549 valid responses are included
in these results.

Key Survey Findings

1. *Social Media Complements Traditional Channels.* Journalists across all three markets were largely in agreement
   that social media sites were an important working tool.
   However, social media is being used in conjunction with
   more traditional sources, such as press releases or direct
   contact with PRs [public relations departments]. Importantly, while social media is playing an increased role in
   the journalist's day-to-day life, personal contacts remain
   one of the leading sources for stories and fact-checking.

2. *Wikipedia Most Used Social Media Source.* Respondents tended to find stories from traditional sources, such as contacts, PRs and corporate sites. They also actively used Wikipedia to source stories, particularly in Germany where use of the site was around twice that seen elsewhere. Wikipedia was also used for fact-checking, with over 60% of respondents using the site to check stories at least once a week, compared to 22% for blogs, or 34% for news wire services.

3. *Journalists Perceive PRs as Not Understanding Social Media.* One-third of respondents in the UK felt that PRs did not understand social media. The journalists' perception is that PRs seldom communicate with them via social platforms, despite their regular use of social media platforms to source stories.

Journalists and Social Media

The wave of search and collaborative ("Web 2.0") technologies that have accompanied the spread of broadband over the past ten years are wholly rewriting the rules of publishing. It has become commonplace for individuals to publish content online, ranging from photos from day-to-day life to world historical events scooped on a mobile phone. At the same time, this proliferation of content, and the changing structures through which it is delivered, have severely undermined the economic foundations of traditional media.

In many respects, the consequences for journalism have been well documented. Newsrooms have been redesigned to better channel online news gathering; while traditional roles have been outsourced, replicated by technology, or demolished outright. The profession as a whole has been subject to extreme cuts, piling pressure on remaining staff.

Yet the intersection of journalism and social media—the ways in which journalists use social media in their work—has been subject to considerably less examination. . . .

Earlier research by Cision North America and Cision Scandinavia firmly suggested the growing significance of social and other digital media in the lives of journalists in these regions. Whether working in ink or pixels, they were clearly using blogs, Twitter and Google. Yet quite how journalists made use of these technologies was not entirely clear. In July 2010, we asked that question directly to journalists in France, Germany, and the UK.

Wikipedia was also used for fact-checking, with over 60% of respondents using the site to check stories at least once a week.

Drawing a sample from the millions of journalists profiled in our media database, we approached journalists across a broad range of media types, interests and locales. Most were aged between 24 and 44, but younger and older age groups were also well represented. A large majority of the respondents had been journalists for more than ten years.

The following provides an overview of the UK results while referencing findings from Germany and France where comparisons were relevant.

The Social Newsroom

Social media are well established as a complementary working utensil for journalists in the UK, Germany and France—but particularly the UK. 74 per cent of the UK journalists said that social media had become an important tool in their work, while in Germany and France a little over 50 per cent thought it important.

It's important to stress that this does not reflect the technographic split of the sample—when asked about the importance of online and social media in their lives, the journalists were more evenly divided, with as many as 50 per cent of

German respondents stating that they were either "unimportant" or somewhat "unimportant" outside the office.

Networking sites such as LinkedIn and Facebook were identified as the single most important social technology for journalism by approximately 30 per cent of UK respondents, with Twitter not far behind. Again, the picture in Germany and France was similar, although French journalists appear comparatively Twitter-verse. Despite this, and the broader range of sites used in France and Germany (XING in Germany, for example), Twitter, LinkedIn and Facebook were the most used platforms in all three countries.

According to our study, there has been a significant increase in journalists' use of social media and search engines over the past three years. However, traditional tools are not being relegated—only a small minority of respondents reported using traditional channels either more or less than they did three years ago. Online tools are supplementing rather than replacing traditional communications.

Our survey firmly suggests that social media's prime purpose in journalism comes in the promotion of [journalists'] work.

Journalists at Work

The [graph] shows the relative proportion of UK respondents using various media and communications tools for sourcing stories more than once a week. At this level, there is an even split between social media and more traditional approaches to sourcing, such as personal contacts, newswires and corporate websites. Search engines remain the key online technology here, with a little over a quarter of UK respondents turning to social channels to source stories.

This picture was remarkably consistent across all three territories, although German use of Wikipedia was around twice that elsewhere. This was a trend repeated through the journalistic process. It is clear from comments made by German respondents that this is not necessarily an issue of greater trust in the online encyclopedia: Most respondents flagged the need to check the validity of Wikipedia entries as much as other social sources.

Differences between social and traditional tools become more apparent when journalists were asked about fact-checking. . . . Here we clearly identify a preference for research and validation through PRs, personal contacts and corporate websites—though again, Wikipedia was more frequently used at this level in Germany than anywhere else.

Our survey firmly suggests that social media's prime purpose in journalism comes in the promotion of [journalists'] work. . . . 54 per cent of UK journalists indicated that microblogging and social networking were among their main channels for distributing their work. There was a greater reliance on social networking in Germany and France, where attitudes toward Twitter appear more suspicious, but the picture was much the same. This self-promotion suggests that the long-standing entrepreneurial nature of journalism is perhaps becoming more pronounced amid the uncertainty that clouds the industry.

Social Media and Public Relations

We asked the journalists to what extent they agreed with the statement that "PRs understand how to use social media". Although 25 per cent of UK respondents believe PRs agreed "somewhat" or "completely", 32 per cent disagreed, suggesting a general perception that PRs lack the knowledge and understanding of social media and how best to use it.

This perception is underscored by the ways in which journalists currently communicate with the PR community.

Traditional channels still dominate this dialogue, with 57 per cent of journalists claiming that PRs still mainly rely on

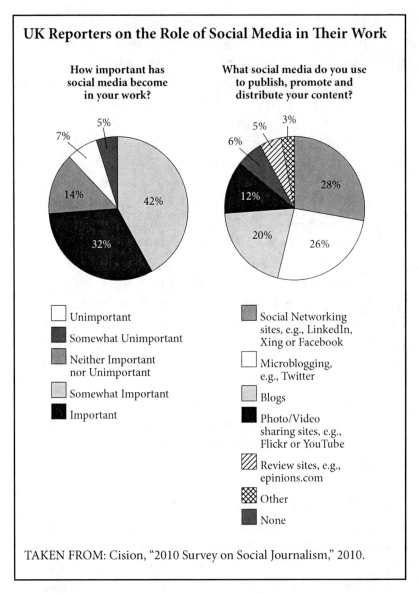

UK Reporters on the Role of Social Media in Their Work

How important has social media become in your work?

- 7%
- 5%
- 42%
- 14%
- 32%

What social media do you use to publish, promote and distribute your content?

- 3%
- 5%
- 6%
- 28%
- 12%
- 20%
- 26%

Legend (left chart):
- ☐ Unimportant
- ■ Somewhat Unimportant
- ▨ Neither Important nor Unimportant
- ▨ Somewhat Important
- ■ Important

Legend (right chart):
- ▨ Social Networking sites, e.g., LinkedIn, Xing or Facebook
- ☐ Microblogging, e.g., Twitter
- ▨ Blogs
- ■ Photo/Video sharing sites, e.g., Flickr or YouTube
- ▨ Review sites, e.g., epinions.com
- ▨ Other
- ■ None

TAKEN FROM: Cision, "2010 Survey on Social Journalism," 2010.

press releases and phone calls. The journalists' perception is that PRs seldom communicate with them via social platforms—much less web/video conferences—in their regular work.

There appears to be a real opportunity for both journalists and PRs to better use social channels. There is certainly considerable appetite among journalists for social media activity. At the same time, it is clear that journalists in all three countries continue to cherish PRs' traditional strengths: providing access to the best contacts and interviews, an in-depth understanding of organisations and their issues, professionalism with a personal touch.

Such skills are very much transferable to the social space. Certainly most journalists would welcome some trustworthy professionalism in social media: 66 per cent of respondents stated that information delivered via social media is slightly or much less reliable than that delivered by other channels, with only 5 per cent considering it more reliable—statistics that go some way toward explaining the journalists' fondness for self-promotion ahead of sourcing and validating. The kind of problems one would expect surfaced in responses from all three countries: lack of accountability, anonymity, and relevance.

But it was also clear that when the source is trusted, social channels are a great way to connect: As one UK respondent said, social media is more reliable "as you're going straight to the source"—a view echoed in all countries.

About the Survey

In July 2010, Cision media research, linked with the University of Sunderland, completed an online survey in the UK, France and Germany simultaneously. The survey was designed to enhance the media industry's understanding of social media uptake and the impact of social media technologies and processes on journalists' work.

Respondents were taken from Cision's media database of more than 1.5 million influencers globally. Country-specific subpanels were set up and 5,000 journalists per country were invited with broad spread of work experience, media types as well as geographies.

Below is an outline of the respondents for each country:

UK	Germany	France
Most respondents aged 24–34, 35–44 but all age groups well represented	Most respondents aged 35–44, 45–54	All ages evenly represented by respondents
	Fewer younger respondents	A large majority have been journalists for more than ten years
A large majority have been journalists for more than ten years	A large majority have been journalists for more than ten years	n = 139
n = 279	n = 131	

Cision will conduct this survey on an annual basis to continue to inform on best practices within the PR and communications field and to deepen the industry's understanding of how journalists and professional communicators use and value social media and other resources.

In the United States, Social Networking Is Helping Military Veterans Recover from Trauma

Matthew M. Burke

Matthew M. Burke is a writer for Stars and Stripes. *In the following viewpoint, he reports on social media communities such as the Wounded Warrior Project that provide resources for veterans. Burke says that veterans are often reluctant to seek help for post-traumatic stress disorder or have trouble negotiating bureaucratic barriers when they do seek help. He says that social networks for veterans can refer veterans quickly to professional resources. Burke reports that veterans are also often helped by being able to talk with other veterans and may find relief in sharing their experiences.*

As you read, consider the following questions:

1. How many followers does the Wounded Warrior Project have, and how many referrals does it make in a typical week?

2. What does Jason Hansman say is the advantage of having a close social media community rather than a Facebook-based community?

Matthew M. Burke, "Social Media Bridging Gap Between Troubled Vets and Treatment," *Stars and Stripes*, September 23, 2011. Used with permission from Stars and Stripes. © 2011, 2013 Stars and Stripes.

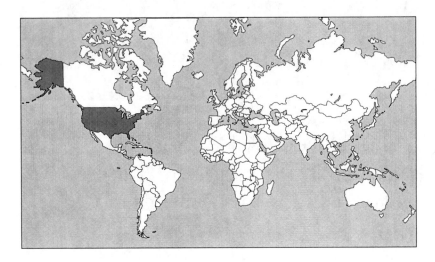

3. According to Burke, how does J.P. Villont use social media?

Marine Cpl. [Corporal] J.P. Villont returned from Iraq a broken man.

The married father of four was angry, paranoid, hypervigilant, aggressive and withdrawn—telltale signs of post-traumatic stress disorder [PTSD].

Seeking Help

Yet, for seven years, the former Marine was reluctant to seek help.

"Obviously I had PTSD and it was undiagnosed," Villont, 40, said recently from his Phoenix home. "It's a huge stigma, so I didn't want to find that out. I pretended I didn't have it for many years."

Then, following a couple of violent outbursts, Villont finally contacted a few veterans facilities in Arizona. He was told he would have to wait months for treatment.

With seemingly nowhere to turn, his wife, Lisa, started posting messages on the Wounded Warrior Project's [WWP's] Facebook page.

"It's been over 7 years since my husband returned home from Iraq, just last week he finally decided to seek help for what we assume will be diagnosed as PTSD," she wrote.

Her words caught the attention of Jennifer Boyce, social media manager for the Wounded Warrior Project, who provided the Villonts with people who could help immediately.

"It sounds like your family is tackling many challenges together," Boyce wrote. "I wanted to let you know that Wounded Warrior Project is here as a resource to help.... I would love to put you in touch with the director of our Combat Stress Recovery Program."

"If we had not encountered [Wounded Warrior Project] ... I would be a widow today."

Lisa Villont is convinced that Boyce's actions helped save her husband's life.

"I can tell you, there is little doubt in my mind that if we had not encountered WWP ... I would be a widow today," Lisa Villont said. "He absolutely, positively, would have found a way to kill himself."

Mental health experts say social media websites are game changers when it comes to reaching out to veterans.

While they shouldn't be viewed as replacements for actual clinical treatment, sites such as Facebook, Twitter, LinkedIn and the Iraq and Afghanistan Veterans of America's "Community of Veterans" are providing veterans and their families with an outlet for referrals, advice and helpful programs, according to the experts. The sites have also become a way for vets to keep in touch and share their experiences with others—something the experts say is invaluable for recovery.

"They Are Not Alone"

At most any hour of the day, Boyce can be found in front of her computer looking for veterans in need of help.

Posts that emphasize struggles with home foreclosures, injuries, thoughts of suicide and symptoms of PTSD are met with a caring note from Boyce and a referral to a professional who might be able to help.

The Wounded Warrior Project Facebook page is one of the most traversed sites for veterans—with about 450,000 followers—and the number of people Boyce has connected with has exploded in the past two years.

"The incredible growth in referral volume has been a bit of a surprise, and it shows no sign of slowing," said Boyce, who has hired a second full-time staffer to help her monitor the site. "There's a great sense of relief when [veterans] learn that we're here to help."

The number of referrals to the proper mental health or counseling professionals can vary, but Boyce said there might be 20–30 referrals in any given week. When the WWP posts something about a specific challenge veterans face, such as PTSD or benefits, the responses increase and can generate 75 to 100 referrals for that single post.

"You'll see with many of them that they are not direct requests for help," Boyce said in reference to the posts. "We find that many veterans are reluctant to seek help for themselves, even if they are struggling. A big part of our referrals are situations like these, where we reach out and say, 'We see you're going through a tough time, and we're here to have your back.' More often than not, a message like that opens up dialogue that ultimately results in warriors connecting with resources that can help."

Through these postings and private messages, military charities and other nonprofit groups can offer veterans access to support—filling a void where local assistance might come up short. And the feedback is almost instantaneous, from administrators like Boyce to other veterans who might have already navigated the murky bureaucratic waters.

Dr. Charles Hoge, author of *Once a Warrior, Always a Warrior*, and the former director of the top U.S. research program in the psychological and neurological consequences of war at Walter Reed Army Institute of Research, has studied and written about the importance of peer-to-peer connections in the recovery process, something nurtured by social media.

"Probably one of the most healing things in PTSD is to talk about your experiences that happened downrange," said Hoge, a retired Army colonel. "There's something very powerful in being able to narrate your experiences while deployed."

That's where sites like the Iraq and Afghanistan Veterans of America [IAVA] can help.

Jason Hansman, IAVA's membership director, manages the Community of Veterans [COV], a social network exclusively for confirmed veterans of the current conflicts. The site boasts 16,000 members.

Unlike the Wounded Warrior Project, the IAVA's Community of Veterans page provides an extra layer of protection from public scrutiny, as many combat veterans only feel comfortable sharing painful secrets with other combat veterans, Hansman said.

"Probably one of the most healing things in PTSD is to talk about your experiences that happened downrange."

"We have seen a lot of people post issues such as unemployment and disability claims to our Facebook and Twitter," he said. "However, on COV we see the relationship issues, the depression and the suicidal ideations. Basically because of the nature of the community and the typical stigma that would be present on Facebook is decreased."

Overcoming Secrecy

Overcoming the sense of shame and secrecy is key to seeking help, said Dr. Glenn Schiraldi, author of *The Resilient Warrior:*

Before, During, and After War, and professor at the University of Maryland School of Public Health.

"An aspect of PTSD is that vets can be very troubled by anything that triggers haunting memories, so they tend to avoid those who talk about war, and even avoid anything that makes them feel," said Schiraldi, a retired Army lieutenant colonel. "On the other hand, once they connect with others [online] they might realize that they are not alone."

But, a few encouraging words on a Facebook page cannot replace the treatment a veteran would receive from a professional counselor, Hoge said.

If social media puts treatment and other resources within a click of the mouse, it definitely has value. Only about 50 percent of veterans who need treatment actually get it, he said, and about half of those drop out.

"In this generation, social media is so important," Hoge said. "There are good treatments out there. Anything that connects [veterans] with others and helps them find things that are useful to them is beneficial."

Veterans just need to be careful.

"It's better to start with established programs like Wounded Warrior Project or one of the other many excellent military and veterans charities," Boyce said. "If a random civilian reaches out to you and offers help, be smart and cautious, just as you would in any other situation."

One Warrior's Story

Finding others with similar problems was the key for J.P. Villont.

In 2003, the infantryman was attached to the 1st Tank Battalion as a machine gunner during the invasion of Iraq. His unit fought its way through Basra, all the way to Baghdad.

"We were in direct combat with the Republican Guard—their tank battalion," the soft-spoken Villont recalled. "I was with 60 tanks so we were rocking and rolling. I saw a lot of destruction."

In the middle of his tour, he went on leave to be with his then pregnant wife who required an emergency surgery in a California hospital.

He rode out of Baghdad with two body bags next to him.

Villont was supposed to have 10 days of leave before heading back to war. But, word came down that his unit had accomplished their mission and that he was no longer needed in Iraq.

"That was pretty surreal," he said. "Like the Vietnam vets, I went directly from combat back into civilian life."

He left the Marines and returned to his job in law enforcement.

Not long after, his troubles began.

First, he assaulted a neighbor who shot bottle rockets toward his home in the middle of the night; Villont said it triggered a flashback. He was later jailed for a morning after a domestic disturbance last year, which triggered a six-month investigation. He was cleared after no charges were filed. He was then allowed back to work.

Although he is not cured, J.P. Villont no longer ruins family outings because of his outbursts.

Finally, he sought help but was unsuccessful, and his wife reached out to the web community.

After reading Lisa Villont's postings, Boyce referred the couple to local services and a Project Odyssey retreat with fellow vets. The retreat offered outdoor activities and the companionship of fellow combat veterans, plus counselors.

At first, Villont resisted. But after talking with other vets, he decided to give it a shot.

"I didn't want to sit around hugging each other singing 'Kumbaya,'" he said. "But it was me and seven other vets. We clicked immediately. It was a breath of life."

Now, J.P. Villont exchanges texts, calls, e-mails and Facebook messages with the other veterans he has met.

He uses social media to monitor legislation and find other outreach organizations, and he received a scholarship from the University of Phoenix to get a master's degree in clinical mental health counseling so he can help other veterans. Villont is retiring from his job as a highway patrolman at the Arizona Department of Public Safety due to injuries from an on-duty crash in March.

Although he is not cured, J.P. Villont no longer ruins family outings because of his outbursts. He's learned he has certain "triggers"—his wife calls it his "Spidey" senses—and needs to stop before he reacts to them, to ask why he feels threatened. Villont just got out of a 24-day inpatient PTSD clinic in Tucson and is looking forward to starting school in October, thanks to the single post his wife made a few months ago.

"It's been a pretty amazing asset," Villont said. "You're able to learn about this stuff from your computer. . . . Once you start opening doors, there is no end to this stuff."

In Canada, Social Media Is Being Explored as a Disaster Warning Device

Janet Davison

Janet Davison is a reporter and writer for CBC, the Canadian news service. In the following viewpoint, she reports that authorities are beginning to use Facebook, Twitter, and other social media outlets to disseminate disaster warnings in Canada. In general, Davison says, the initial disaster alert is not issued through social media, but follow-up alerts and information may be. Davison says that one problem with social media for alerts is that not everyone is connected to social media. However, she reports that authorities are realizing that it is important to get reliable information out through social media to counter misleading reports that may be circulating.

As you read, consider the following questions:

1. What Canadian disaster does Davison discuss in which she suggests that social media warnings might have been helpful?
2. What are three examples that Davison provides of Canadian government and weather organizations that use social media for warnings?

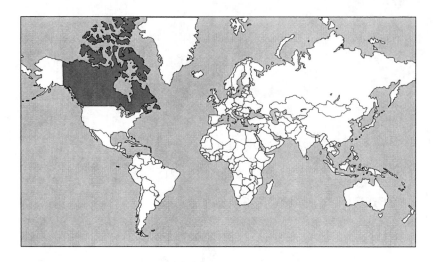

3. According to Davison, how does Mexico City currently alert residents during emergencies, and what new techniques is the city considering?

When wind-whipped wildfires were bearing down on Slave Lake, Alta., [Alberta] 10 days ago [in May 2011], residents had little advance warning to get out of town. Eventually, an evacuation order was given, but by that point the town's radio station was burning and roads coming and going from Slave Lake were shut down.

Turning to Twitter

Provincial officials said the fire was moving so fast it was impossible to issue a bulletin through their public warning system. Police went knocking on doors to warn residents. But for many worried evacuees, information they could use wasn't coming through traditional channels like radio or TV.

"We'd check the Facebook quite a bit," resident Anthony Cyr said. "Cell phones were spotty, too, but the texting was working OK."

As has been happening during so many other natural disasters or public demonstrations around the world, social media became a go-to source of information and a place for those on the ground to share with others what they knew about a tense situation.

But what about before the fires actually hit Slave Lake? Could timely messages from authorities via Facebook or Twitter have helped alert or warn residents?

Social Media Can Disseminate Vital Information

Government and weather organizations in Canada are using social media to provide updates and information. Here's a sampling:

- The Weather Network has a number of provincial Twitter feeds, where they post regional watches and warnings.

- The Canadian Avalanche Association started tweeting last winter. It sends out alerts and also shares people's avalanche reports.

- The New Brunswick emergency management office recently started tweeting.

- Alberta wildfire management has a Twitter account it uses to update the status of current fires.

- B.C.'s wildfire management has a Twitter account that it used to provide flood information this spring.

As has been happening during so many other natural disasters or public demonstrations around the world, social media became a go-to source of information.

Disaster sociologist Jeannette Sutton, who studies the role online technologies can play in a disaster, says social media is now being explored as a warning device.

"It is understudied because it is a pretty new idea," she said in an e-mail Wednesday.

Sutton, who works at the University of Colorado in Colorado Springs, doesn't look to social media for issuing the initial alert.

She does, however, see it as a useful tool for providing people with information after that initial alert, particularly for people who are already online.

Social Media as a Secondary Warning System

"For a warning system, social media can be very useful, especially for the ability to monitor what people are saying and doing in response to the alerts they receive."

Sutton recognizes, however, there could be fears or concerns about using social media as a warning system.

"Technology is not a silver bullet. And social media is just one tool in the tool kit. You can't rely entirely on this technology."

For one thing, not everyone has a Twitter or Facebook account or access to a computer or cell phone.

But around the world, some communities are looking to social media as one way of alerting residents to imminent disasters. Mexico City wants to set up an earthquake alert system through social networking sites such as Facebook and Twitter.

Mayor Marcelo Ebrard said earlier this month he hopes to have the system working by Sept. 19, the anniversary of an 8.1-magnitude earthquake in 1985 that killed as many as 10,000 people.

Mexico City currently has an early warning system that uses sirens to alert city residents about quakes that occur hundreds of kilometres away on Pacific coast fault lines. Some people complain the alarms in their neighbourhoods can't be heard or don't go off.

Social Media and the 2008 Burma Cyclone

On May 2, 2008, Cyclone Nargis struck the Irrawaddy Delta region of Myanmar (Burma). The cyclone, with winds of 120 mph, made landfall at the mouth of the Irrawaddy River—a low-lying, densely populated region—and pushed a 12-foot wall of water 25 miles inland, killing at least 80,000 people and leaving as many as 2.5 million homeless. Ten days later, on May 12, 2008, a 7.9 earthquake devastated China's Sichuan province, toppling buildings, collapsing schools, killing more than 69,000, injuring over 367,000, and displacing between 5 and 11 million people. . . .

In Myanmar, where Internet and cell phone access is limited, the military government refused to allow aid workers or journalists to reach disaster areas and moved fast to restrict communications. Ironically, it was a local online news source . . . that reported on the "guidelines" the junta had laid out for journalists' coverage, specifically prohibiting showing dead bodies or reporting about insufficient aid for victims.

In spite of these restrictions, Burmese blogs and news sites were quick to react by posting eyewitness accounts of the disaster and mobilizing fund-raising efforts. According to BBC News, "People inside Burma have been giving their updates from the disaster zone. Burmese blogger Nyi Lynn Seck has a section of his blog devoted to daily updates from the Delta region. . . ."

In addition to the news gathering done by citizen journalists online (bloggers), other new media technologies helped tell the story of the Burmese disaster and recovery.

George D. Haddow, Jane A. Bullock, and Damon P. Coppola,
Introduction to Emergency Management.
4th ed. Burlington, MA: Butterworth-Heinemann, 2011, pp. 149–150.

The Philippine government is also encouraging the use of social media as a disaster warning tool.

Across Canada, municipal governments are on the front lines for helping residents deal with disasters, while provincial governments generally have overall responsibility for emergency response.

TV and Radio Warning Systems

In Alberta, for example, the provincial Emergency Public Warning System was set up after the 1987 Edmonton tornado to give "warning to Albertans over the radio and the television to take action and protect themselves from disasters," according to its website. "This system is activated by trained users living throughout Alberta who, using their telephone, will deliver vital information regarding a threat to the safety of Albertans."

In Ontario, the province's Emergency Public Warning System includes Red Alerts and Emergency Information Advisories.

The Red Alert program was launched three years ago, and is based on the AMBER Alert program for missing children.

Red Alerts are issued "when there is an imminent threat to life, public safety or property," according to Emergency Management Ontario's [EMO's] website. They could be issued in situations such as a large fire or explosion, a chemical leak or spill, a nuclear emergency, an extreme weather event or a transportation accident. The alerts are posted on the EMO website and distributed through media outlets, an e-mail subscriber service, text messaging, RSS feed and Twitter.

Emergency Information Advisories are issued in situations such as large-scale power outages or major transportation incidents and distributed in ways similar to Red Alerts.

In Edmonton, emergency officials have a presence on social media sites, but don't use it as their primary warning system, says Joanne Sheardown, an emergency management officer for the city.

"There's still a part of the population that doesn't sign up for Facebook or Twitter."

Rather, Facebook and Twitter are used to get out updates to Edmonton residents after any initial warning.

Providing "Reliable Information"

The city made its foray into the social media world a couple of years ago after a series of large windstorms. Suddenly Edmonton and its weather situation became one of the top 10 trending topics on Twitter worldwide.

"I think you need to get your messaging out in as many different ways as possible because there [are] so many different audiences out there who retrieve information differently."

"We wanted to make sure that we were providing reliable information so if someone was re-tweeting messages, they were re-tweeting our messages and not rumours," says Sheardown.

With the rapidly evolving nature of communication, and the way people get their information, Sheardown sees much virtue in being active on Facebook and Twitter.

"I think you need to get your messaging out in as many different ways as possible because there [are] so many different audiences out there who retrieve information differently," she said.

And that means looking ahead, too.

"We need to start planning now for incorporating these tools into our public information campaigns in the future," said Sheardown.

Ultimately, she expects Facebook and Twitter will be used for getting warnings out.

"We're not all there yet."

When Chávez Tweets, Venezuelans Listen

Ezequiel Minaya and Kejal Vyas

Ezequiel Minaya and Kejal Vyas are reporters for the Dow Jones newswire and contributors to the Wall Street Journal. *In the following viewpoint, they report that Hugo Chávez, the president of Venezuela, has made extensive use of Twitter to keep in touch with his citizens. Chávez has been receiving cancer treatments in Cuba, they report, and he has tweeted constantly, even making policy declarations by Twitter. The authors say Twitter is useful for Chávez because it allows him to update followers on his health and policy without facing journalistic questioning. Still, the authors report, governing by Twitter is not feasible, and Chávez still has to make public appearances on occasion.*

As you read, consider the following questions:

1. Why do the authors say that Twitter has taken on added importance for Chávez?

2. How many Twitter followers does Chávez have, and how does that compare to the president of Brazil?

3. Who is Henrique Capriles, according to the authors?

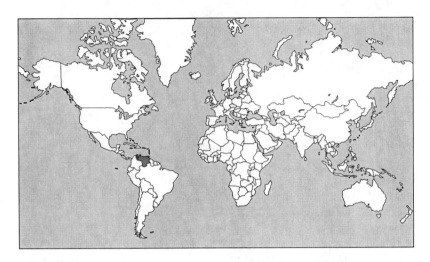

Venezuela president Hugo Chávez, who is notorious for long-winded and rambling speeches, has taken his garrulous style online—and in short form.

During his latest stay in Cuba for cancer treatment, the leader has made Twitter his nearly exclusive means of public communication. It turns out Mr. Chávez on Twitter is much like Mr. Chávez in the flesh.

His tweets come in a torrent, with a striking irreverence for a head of state. Recently he posted a message celebrating his lunch of plantains, rice and "tremendous" fish soup. He casually delivers news of government policy shifts and project approvals. Virtually all his tweets are punctuated with exclamation points.

"Comrades you make me very happy!" he tweeted on Saturday. "Let's keep fighting hard to defeat the bourgeoisie! It is pouring in Havana and I am with you!"

The social networking site has taken on an added importance in recent days, as Mr. Chávez tries to counter rumors of failing health and keep a presence with Venezuelan voters, some of whom question his future in office ahead of elections this fall.

With Mr. Chávez in Cuba since April 14 completing radiation therapy for an undisclosed type of cancer, Venezuela's unpredictable presidential contest has been fought in online volleys of 140 characters or less. The country's opposition has accused the president of governing via Twitter—in tweets of its own.

"Chávez has been compulsive in seizing whatever means, like Twitter, to manage his own image," said Xavier Rodríguez, a political scientist at Simón Bolívar University in Caracas.

It turns out that Mr. Chávez on Twitter is much like Mr. Chávez in the flesh.

Calls to Venezuela's minister of information Andrés Izarra, who is widely seen as a main architect of the government's social media use, especially Twitter, weren't returned.

The media-savvy president has minimized public appearances during his stint in Cuba, where he has received most of his treatment in near secret. Mr. Chávez has shuttled between Caracas and Havana since June, when doctors in Cuba removed a malignant tumor from his pelvic region. Surgeons extracted a new growth two months ago.

The Venezuelan leader, who launched his Twitter account in 2010, has hired a staff to respond to tweets he receives. It is unclear whether he writes all his own missives, but they do sound just like Mr. Chávez speaking.

But he barrages his 2.8 million Twitter followers, which amount to about twice as many as Brazilian president Dilma Rousseff, a less active tweeter.

Mr. Chávez directs cheerful messages to his ministers and re-election campaign aides to express approval for their efforts. He comments on the weather or sporting events and announces the passing of legislation. He often rallies his supporters to push forward his socialist "21st century Bolivarian Revolution."

Hugo Chávez

Venezuelan president Hugo Chávez and his policies have sparked controversy at home, throughout the Latin American region, and in the United States. . . . Chávez, however, has stayed in power through democratic means and carries overwhelming support, despite large-scale attempts to remove him from office. . . .

Chávez first gained national attention in 1992 when he led an unsuccessful military coup to oust President Carlos Andrés Pérez. . . .

By 1994 Chávez had transformed from a "military rebel to a democratic player". He founded the political party Movement of the Fifth Republic leading up to the 1998 presidential elections. His platform emphasized his desire to end corruption, return oil to state control, and eliminate poverty. This platform earned him political victory in 1998 with 56 percent of the vote, in 2000 with 60.3 percent, and in 2006 with 63 percent. . . .

Chávez's mass appeal remains debatable. Scholars and journalists attribute his success to his emphasis on the country's poor through health and education programs. . . .

However, critics argue that the statistics contradict the myth. Francisco Rodríguez argues that social spending in Venezuela decreased from 31.5 percent prior to Chávez's administration to 29.3 percent by 2004. . . . Instead, Chávez's popularity is based on the country's double-digit economic growth, according to Rodriguez. . . .

As of 2007, Venezuela's economy remained stable while a large number of Venezuelans lived in deep poverty. Nevertheless, Chávez's support surpassed that of his critics.

"Chávez, Hugo," International Encyclopedia of the Social Sciences, *ed. William A. Darity Jr., 2nd ed., vol. 1. Detroit, MI: Macmillan Reference USA, 2008, pp. 494–495.*

After not being seen or heard from for more than a week, apart from his tweets, Mr. Chávez's flurry didn't stop a rumor from spreading over the weekend that he had died. To quash the speculation, Mr. Chávez telephoned a state television station on Monday, and followed that Tuesday with a video showing the 57-year-old leader in a blue and white track suit, lawn bowling with his aides.

Mr. Chávez's heavy reliance on Twitter has raised the status of social media for Venezuelans, who voraciously seek out information on the president's health.

Internet researcher comScore Inc. estimates Venezuela has the world's fourth-highest concentration of Twitter users. It was used by 29% of Venezuelans with Internet access in March. That number, which doesn't include users who log on through smartphones, still puts Venezuela on the level of countries such as the U.S., U.K. and Canada, per capita.

While the medium has given Mr. Chávez the ability to directly address his followers, the openness of the social network has also left him vulnerable to easily spread rumors about his cancer, experts said.

Mr. Chávez's heavy reliance on Twitter has raised the status of social media for Venezuelans, who voraciously seek out information on the president's health.

"You can't understand the impact of Twitter in Venezuela until you understand that the national sport is gossiping," said Antonio Cova, a sociology professor at the Central University of Venezuela in Caracas. "And the dessert of the day is the health of the very president of the country."

Opposition presidential candidate, Miranda state governor Henrique Capriles, who is seen as having the strongest chance of unseating Mr. Chávez after 13 years in office, chimed in with his own tweets Sunday.

Mr. Capriles, who has nearly 781,000 followers on Twitter, criticized Mr. Chávez for effectively running the government through Twitter.

"Twitter is a type of communication that people who want to avoid critical media really like."

During his telephone comments Monday, Mr. Chávez replied that accusing him of governing via Twitter was "absurd," noting that such communications are "strategies to govern."

Silvio Waisbord, an associate director of the School of Media and Public Affairs at George Washington University, said the Chávez administration is far ahead of other governments in Latin America in its embrace of social media.

Twitter "fits Chávez like a glove," Mr. Waisbord said. "Twitter is a type of communication that people who want to avoid critical media really like. You don't have anyone asking questions. You can make the argument that one should not govern by Twitter. But why would Chávez shut up on Twitter if he's so aggressive on every other type of media?"

Still, "what cannot happen is that you only communicate through social networks," said Guillermo Amador, director of local social media consultancy DosPuntoUno in Caracas. "In the end, there has to be some physical contact."

Periodical and Internet Sources Bibliography

The following articles have been selected to supplement the diverse views presented in this chapter.

Arlina Arshad — "Smartphones, Social Media Help in Tsunami Warnings," ABS-CBNNews.com, April 12, 2012.

Bob Brewin — "VA Promotes Social Media Use with New Policy," Nextgov, August 16, 2011. www.nextgov.com.

Mercedes Bunz — "Most Journalists Use Social Media Such as Twitter and Facebook as a Source," *Guardian*, February 15, 2010.

Clare Kermond — "Tourism Australia Turns Marketing Focus to Social Media," *Sydney Morning Herald*, January 12, 2012.

John Liebhardt — "Can Social Media Help Make Microfinance Sustainable?," Global Voices, September 21, 2009. http://globalvoicesonline.org.

Margaret Looney — "How Reuters Journalists Use Social Media," IJNET, April 17, 2012. http://ijnet.org.

Samantha Murphy — "Iceland's Social Media Efforts Help Inspire Tourism Bump," TechNewsDaily, November 9, 2011. www.technewsdaily.com.

Abigail Phillips — "Social Media Is Key in Building Customer Relationships," Business Review Europe, November 17, 2011. www.businessreview europe.eu.

Mike Snider — "Social Media Is Latest Front of Cola Wars," *USA Today*, April 29, 2012.

CHAPTER 3

Social Networking and Democratic Movements

Worldwide, Social Networking May Help Authoritarian Regimes More than It Helps Democratic Movements

The Economist

The Economist *is a British newsmagazine that covers business and politics. In the following viewpoint, the* Economist *reviews Evgeny Morozov's book* The Net Delusion: The Dark Side of Internet Freedom, *in which he argues that the Internet is not inherently democratic. According to the* Economist, *Morozov points out that Internet entertainment can distract people from politics. He also says that authoritarian regimes can use social media to track dissidents or to spread official government propaganda. Morozov, according to the* Economist, *argues that the West's belief that the Internet always promotes democracy makes it hard for governments to react intelligently to authoritarian uses of social media. Thus, he maintains, a belief in the democratizing effects of social media can actually hurt democracy.*

As you read, consider the following questions:

1. What evidence does the *Economist* cite to show that the Iranian protests were not a Twitter revolution?

The Economist, "Politics and the Internet: Caught in the Net," January 6, 2011. © The Economist Newspaper Limited, London 2011.

2. According to the *Economist*, what was the effect of allowing East Germans to watch soap operas during the Communist dictatorship?

3. Why does Morozov believe it is implausible to describe one Internet approach to use against all authoritarian regimes?

When thousands of young Iranians took to the streets in June 2009 to protest against the apparent rigging of the presidential election, much of the coverage in the Western media focused on the protesters' use of Twitter, a microblogging service, "This would not happen without Twitter," declared the *Wall Street Journal*. Andrew Sullivan, a prominent American-based blogger, also proclaimed Twitter to be "the critical tool for organising the resistance in Iran". The *New York Times* said the demonstrations pitted "thugs firing bullets" against "protestors firing tweets".

"Cyber-Utopian" Delusion

The idea that the Internet was fomenting revolution and promoting democracy in Iran was just the latest example of the widely held belief that communications technology, and the Internet in particular, is inherently pro-democratic. In this gleefully iconoclastic book [*The Net Delusion: The Dark Side of Internet Freedom*], Evgeny Morozov takes a stand against this "cyber-utopian" view, arguing that the Internet can be just as effective at sustaining authoritarian regimes. By assuming that the Internet is always pro-democratic, he says, Western policy makers are operating with a "voluntary intellectual handicap" that makes it harder rather than easier to promote democracy.

He starts with the events in Iran, which illustrate his argument in microcosm. An investigation by Al Jazeera, an international news network based in Qatar, could confirm only 60 active Twitter accounts in Tehran [the capital of Iran]. Iranian bloggers who took part in the protests have since poured cold water on the "Twitter revolution" theory. But the American government's endorsement of the theory, together with the State Department's request that Twitter delay some planned maintenance that would have taken the service off-line for a few crucial hours at the height of the unrest, prompted the Iranian authorities to crack down on social networks of all kinds. Iranians entering the country were, for example, looked up on Facebook to see if they had links to any known dissidents, thus achieving the very opposite of what American policy makers wanted.

The root of the problem, Mr Morozov argues, is that Western policy makers see an all-too-neat parallel with the role that radio propaganda and photocopiers may have played in undermining the Soviet Union. A native of Belarus, Mr Morozov (who has occasionally written for the *Economist*) says this oversimplification of history has led to the erroneous conclusion that promoting Internet access and "Internet freedom" will have a similar effect on authoritarian regimes today.

By assuming that the Internet is always pro-democratic, . . . Western policy makers are operating with a "voluntary intellectual handicap."

Internet as Pacification

In fact, authoritarian regimes can use the Internet, as well as greater access to other kinds of media, such as television, to their advantage. Allowing East Germans to watch American soap operas on West German television, for example, seems to have acted as a form of pacification that actually reduced people's interest in politics. Surveys found that East Germans with access to Western television were less likely to express dissatisfaction with the regime. As one East German dissident lamented, "the whole people could leave the country and move to the West as a man at 8pm, via television."

Mr Morozov catalogues many similar examples of the Internet being used with similarly pacifying consequences today, as authoritarian regimes make an implicit deal with their populations: help yourselves to pirated films, silly video clips and online pornography, but stay away from politics. "The Internet," Mr Morozov argues, "has provided so many cheap and easily available entertainment fixes to those living under authoritarianism that it has become considerably harder to get people to care about politics at all."

Social networks offer a cheaper and easier way to identify dissidents than other, more traditional forms of surveillance. Despite talk of a "dictator's dilemma", censorship technology is sophisticated enough to block politically sensitive material without impeding economic activity, as China's example shows. The Internet can be used to spread propaganda very effectively, which is why Hugo Chávez is on Twitter. The web can also be effective in supporting the government line, or at least casting doubt on critics' position (China has an army of pro-government bloggers). Indeed, under regimes where nobody believes the official media, pro-government propaganda spread via the Internet is actually perceived by many to be more credible by comparison.

Social networks offer a cheaper and easier way to identify dissidents than other, more traditional forms of surveillance.

Authoritarian governments are assumed to be clueless about the Internet, but they often understand its political uses far better than their Western counterparts do, Mr Morozov suggests. His profiles in *The Net Delusion* of the Russian government's young Internet advisers are particularly illuminating. Previous technologies, including the telegraph, aircraft, radio and television, were also expected to bolster democracy, he observes, but they failed to live up to expectations. The

Maria Sergeyeva Helps Kremlin Look Cool

The most remarkable character [among the pro-Kremlin Internet gurus] is Maria Sergeyeva, a twenty-five-year-old member of Young Guard, one of the Kremlin's [that is, the Russian government's] pocket youth organizations.

Sergeyeva, a stunning blonde and a student of philosophy, writes a very popular personal blog in which she ruminates about the need to support the dying Russian auto industry, extols Catherine the Great, tells all immigrants to "go home," and occasionally posts photos from the coolest parties around town. "I was brought up to be a patriot from day one," she said in an interview with the *Times* of London. "My love for Russia came with my mother's milk. I loved listening to my grandparents' heroic tales from the war. [Russian president Vladimir] Putin has given us stability and economic growth. It's good that he's hard-line and tough." . . .

The Kremlin badly needs people like Sergeyeva to reach younger audiences that are unreachable via the platforms the government already controls—radio, television, and newspapers. Bringing the young people back into the Kremlin's sway—in part, by making the Kremlin look "cool"—is such a high priority that in 2009 Vladimir Putin, in his address to a national hip-hop convention, proclaimed that "break dancing, hip-hop and graffiti" are more entertaining than "vodka, caviar and nesting dolls."

Evgeny Morozov,
The Net Delusion: The Dark Side of Internet Freedom.
New York: PublicAffairs, 2011, pp. 126–127.

proliferation of channels means that Americans watch less TV news than they did in the pre-cable era. And by endorsing

Twitter, Facebook and Google as pro-democratic instruments, the American government has compromised their neutrality and encouraged authoritarian regimes to regard them as agents of its foreign policy.

"Cyber-Realism"

So what does Mr Morozov propose instead of the current approach? He calls for "cyber-realism" to replace "cyber-utopianism", making it clear that he believes that technology can indeed be used to promote democracy, provided it is done in the right way. But he presents little in the way of specific prescriptions, other than to stress the importance of considering the social and political context in which technology is deployed, rather than focusing on the characteristics of the technology itself, as Internet gurus tend to. Every authoritarian regime is different, he argues, so it is implausible that the same approach will work in each case; detailed local knowledge is vital. Yet having done such a good job of knocking down his opponents' arguments, it is a pity he does not have more concrete proposals to offer in their place.

With chapter titles and headings such as "Why the KGB wants you to join Facebook" and "Why Kierkegaard Hates Slacktivism" it is clear that Mr Morozov is enjoying himself (indeed, there may be a few more bad jokes than is strictly necessary). But the resulting book is not just unfailingly readable: It is also a provocative, enlightening and welcome riposte to the cyber-utopian worldview.

Social Networking Was Important in, Though Not Solely Responsible for, Tunisia's Revolution

Ethan Zuckerman

Ethan Zuckerman is a senior researcher at the Berkman Center for Internet and Society, as well as a cofounder of Global Voices. In the following viewpoint, he argues that social media had an effect on the Tunisian revolution of 2011. He says that social media helped distribute news of protests, encouraging others to take to the streets. In addition, Internet censorship was one of the grievances that galvanized protestors. However, Zuckerman says that the Tunisian revolution was not directly caused by Twitter or other social media. The main cause of the Tunisian uprising, he argues, was long-standing frustration with the dictatorial, corrupt Tunisian government.

As you read, consider the following questions:

1. What concessions does Zuckerman say Ben Ali offered to his people as the protests intensified?
2. Why were video-sharing sites a special target of government censorship in Tunisia, according to Zuckerman?

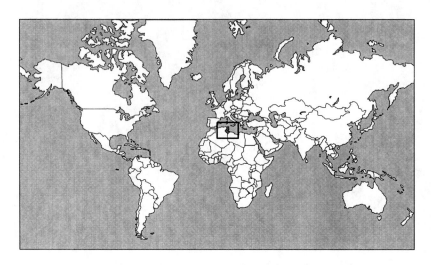

3. What dreaded phrase does Zuckerman accuse Andrew
Sullivan of reviving in reference to Tunisia?

Friday evening [in January 2011], Tunisian president Zine
El Abidine Ben Ali boarded a jet for Malta, leaving his
prime minister to face streets filled with protesters demanding
a change of government in the North African country. The
protests began weeks earlier in the central city of Sidi Bouzid,
sparked by the suicide of Mohamed Bouazizi, an unemployed
university graduate whose informal vegetable stall was shut-
tered by the police. His despair exemplified the frustration
that many Tunisians felt with their contracting economy, high
levels of unemployment and inequality, censored media and
Internet, and widespread corruption. Protests spread from city
to city, with trade unions, lawyers, and countless unemployed
Tunisian youth demanding a change to an economic system
that appeared to benefit a small number of families close to
power and leaving ordinary citizens behind.

Tunisia Without Ben Ali

As the protests intensified, Ben Ali offered concessions to his
people: 23 years into his reign, he agreed to step down in
2014. He ordered the security police to stop using live ammu-

nition on protesters after nearly 70 had been killed, cut the price of basic foodstuffs, and promised to allow a freer media and end Internet censorship. This morning, as pressures increased, he offered new elections within six months. But all that failed to placate the crowds, who finally got what they wanted later in the day: a Tunisia sans Ben Ali.

While the future of Tunisia's governance is extremely uncertain at present, it seems we've witnessed the rarest of phenomena, a popular revolt toppling an Arab dictator. Audiences in the Arab world have been glued to Al Jazeera [a Middle East news network], which has covered the protests closely. Many states in the region suffer from the same problems—unemployment, slow growth, corrupt government, aging dictators—that brought Tunisians into the streets. Protesters have taken to the streets in Algeria and Jordan, demanding jobs and affordable food. Whether these protests erupt into the revolution Tunisia is experiencing is impossible to know. What's clear is that the actions taken by Tunisians are reverberating around the region.

It seems we've witnessed the rarest of phenomena, a popular revolt toppling an Arab dictator.

Outside the Middle East and the Francophone media sphere, the events in Tunisia have gotten little attention, certainly not the breathless, 24-hour coverage devoted to 2009's Iranian election protests. When the protests began in Sidi Bouzid, much of the English-speaking world was focused on the Christmas and New Year's holidays. As protests in Tunis [the capital of Tunisia] heated up, U.S. eyeballs were focused on the tragic shooting in Tucson, Arizona [of U.S. representative Gabrielle Giffords]. Had the Tunisian protests hit during a slow news month, it's still unlikely they would have been followed as closely as events in Iran, which is larger, of greater

91

international security concern, and has a large, media-savvy diaspora who helped promote the 2009 protests to an international audience.

One way to understand the significance of social media in Tunisia is to examine the government's attempt to control and silence it.

Iran's diaspora was especially effective at promoting the green movement to an online audience that followed tweets, Facebook posts, and web videos avidly, hungry for news from the front lines of the struggle. Tens of thousands of Twitter users turned their profile pictures green in solidarity with the activists, and hundreds set up proxy servers to help Iranians evade Internet filters. For users of social media, the protests in Iran were an inescapable, global story. Tunisia, by contrast, hasn't seen nearly the attention or support from the online community.

Twitter, Facebook, and Tunisia

The irony is that social media likely played a significant role in the events that have unfolded in the past month in Tunisia, and that the revolution appears far more likely to lead to lasting political change. Ben Ali's government tightly controlled all forms of media, on and off-line. Reporters were prevented from traveling to cover protests in Sidi Bouzid, and the reports from official media characterized events as either vandalism or terrorism. Tunisians got an alternative picture from Facebook, which remained uncensored through the protests, and they communicated events to the rest of the world by posting videos to YouTube and Dailymotion. As unrest spread from Sidi Bouzid to Sfax, from Hammamet and ultimately to Tunis, Tunisians documented events on Facebook. As others followed their updates, it's likely that news of demonstrations in other parts of the country disseminated online helped others conclude that it was time to take to the streets. And the videos and accounts published to social media sites offered an ongoing picture of the protests to those around the world savvy enough to be paying attention.

One way to understand the significance of social media in Tunisia is to examine the government's attempts to control and silence it. Tunisia has aggressively censored the Internet since 2005, blocking not just explicitly political sites, but social media sites like video-sharing service Dailymotion. Video-sharing sites were a special target of government censors because Tunisian activists are extremely tech savvy and had released provocative videos online, including one that documented the first lady's frequent shopping trips to Europe using the presidential jet.

Tunisians took to the streets due to decades of frustration, not in reaction to a WikiLeaks Cable . . . or a Facebook update.

Not content just to filter content, last summer Tunisian authorities began "phishing" attacks on activists' Gmail and Facebook accounts. By injecting malicious computer code into the log-in page of those services through the government-controlled Internet service provider, Ben Ali's monitors were able to obtain passwords to these accounts, locking out the activists and harvesting e-mail lists of presumed activists. When the riots intensified last week, the government began arresting prominent Internet activists, including my Global Voices colleague Slim Amamou, who had broken the story of the government's password phishing. (Amamou was released, apparently unharmed, Thursday night.)

But if the web was such a threat to the government's authority, why did the regime not block Facebook or shut down the Internet entirely? It's critical to understand that Ben Ali was, first and foremost, a pragmatist. As late as Friday morning, he was looking for a solution that would allow him to remain in power, offering concessions in the hope of placating protesters. Internet censorship was already one of the grievances protesters had aired—when Ben Ali offered concessions to protesters Thursday, loosening the reins was one of the promises that were warmly, if skeptically received.

The Real Cause of Revolution

Pundits will likely start celebrating a "Twitter revolution" in Tunisia, even if they missed watching it unfold; the *Atlantic*'s Andrew Sullivan already revived the dreaded phrase Thursday. Others are seeking connections between unfolding events and a WikiLeaks cable that showed U.S. diplomats' frustration with Ben Ali, and with denial-of-service attacks by online activist group Anonymous, which has been targeting entities that have tried to stop the dissemination of WikiLeaks cables, like the Tunisian government. But any attempt to credit a massive political shift to a single factor—technological, economic, or otherwise—is simply untrue. Tunisians took to the streets due to decades of frustration, not in reaction to a WikiLeaks cable, a denial-of-service attack, or a Facebook update.

But as we learn more about the events of the past few weeks, we'll discover that online media did play a role in helping Tunisians learn about the actions their fellow citizens were taking and in making the decision to mobilize. How powerful and significant this influence was will be something that academics will study and argue over for years to come. Scholars aren't the only ones who want to know whether social media played a role in the end of Ben Ali's reign—it's likely to be a hot topic of conversation in Amman [Jordan], Algiers [Algeria], and Cairo [Egypt], as other autocratic leaders wonder whether the bubbling cauldron of unemployment, street protests, and digital media could burn them next.

Social Networking Has Opened Singapore to Democracy

Raymond Tham

Raymond Tham is a writer and social media manager at Econo mywatch.com. In the following viewpoint, he says that the Singapore government has long restricted free speech as well as terrorized and imprisoned critics. However, he says that has changed with the advent of social media, which have allowed many people to criticize the regime. He notes that anti-regime sentiment online is so great that those who support the regime online are often ostracized. He argues that the Singapore government has actually done a good job of guiding the economy, even though it has lost touch with the needs and goals of everyday Singaporeans. Tham concludes that the new freedom of social media will have an important effect on Singapore's future.

As you read, consider the following questions:

1. What does Tham say was the biggest fear of Singaporeans during the May 2011 general elections in Singapore?
2. According to Tham, who is Wendy Cheng, and what was the controversy surrounding her?

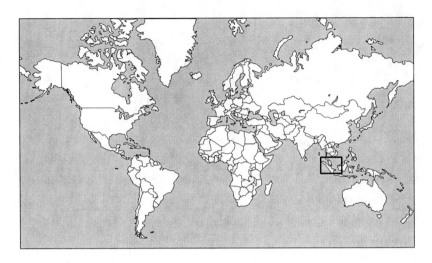

3. How does Singapore rank as an oil exporter, and why does Tham suggest that this is surprising?

I t takes a brave person to write about politics in Singapore.

Fear of the Government

Over the years, publications and journalists have been sued—and even jailed for criticising the ruling People's Action Party (PAP), who have been in power since 1963.

The older generation of Singaporeans believe criticising the government only means trouble. Even in private conversations, many older Singaporeans resist talking about the government in the fear "big brother" may be listening.

In past interviews, former prime minister and founder of the PAP Lee Kuan Yew has made no attempt to mask the fact that his government has deliberately bred a culture of fear within the Singaporean society.

"I have never been over-concerned or obsessed with opinion polls or popularity polls. I think a leader who is, is a weak leader," Lee wrote in his autobiography published in 1997.

"Between being loved and being feared, I have always believed Machiavelli was right. If nobody is afraid of me, I'm meaningless."

Yet surprisingly in the buildup and aftermath of the 2011 Singapore general elections held on the 7th of May, Singaporeans were not afraid to criticise the PAP openly and in media. Instead, the biggest fear was publishing anything that could be construed to support the PAP.

Lee Kuan Yew has made no attempt to mask the fact that his government has deliberately bred a culture of fear within the Singaporean society.

The Social Media Revolution in Singapore

The 2011 Singapore general elections were a watershed event in Singapore's political history. Not because for the first time ever an opposition party (the Workers' Party or WP) managed to secure a Group Representation Constituency (GRC) from the PAP. Nor was it because the PAP's popular vote had fallen from 67 percent in 2007 to 60.1 percent.

Rather, it was a result of Singapore's political landscape being dramatically altered with the advent of social media and the Internet.

The Internet and social media sparked a new way of thinking for Singapore, especially in the political arena. While older Singaporeans relied on state-controlled media agencies for their news and information, the Internet opened up a source of independent information that could not be tightly regulated or controlled as traditional media platforms.

Singapore's Press Freedom Index ranking is a dismal 136th out of 178 countries (assessed by Reporters Without Borders) and 151st out of 196 countries according to the Freedom of the Press 2010 global rankings report.

As Singaporeans began to seek alternative viewpoints that were not expressed in the local media, websites like the Te-

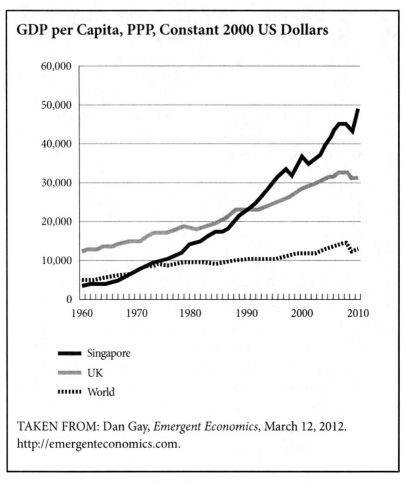

GDP per Capita, PPP, Constant 2000 US Dollars

TAKEN FROM: Dan Gay, *Emergent Economics*, March 12, 2012. http://emergenteconomics.com.

masek Review and The Online Citizen cropped up. These sites gained popularity and support for publishing articles that were critical of the local government for the first time.

Soon, the Internet became a platform for Singaporeans to not only vent their frustrations at the PAP, but also share political opinion and connect with other like-minded individuals.

Despite representing the dawn of a new age of political awareness in Singapore, social media was also responsible for a level of hypocrisy that began to spread as effortlessly as the original call for political change among Singaporeans online.

Anti-PAP sentiments on Facebook and Twitter had reached such incredible heights that people who "dared to criticise the opposition" or advocate the capabilities of the PAP, would be ostracised by the online community.

Moh Hon Meng wrote on his Facebook note entitled "In Defence of the PAP," "When did this happen? It used to be that if you spoke up against the PAP, you feared for your life. But now online sentiment for the PAP has turned so over-whelmingly negative that I'm afraid to post this!"

The Internet and social media sparked a new way of thinking for Singapore, especially in the political arena.

Similarly, popular local blogger Wendy Cheng, a.k.a. Xiaxue, was "flamed" by the online community after she had expressed support for the PAP on her online blog. The online resentment towards her was so intense that advertisers had to pull their ads from her blog in order to avoid any potential backlash.

So what is the irony of it all?

Well on one hand, Singaporeans have complained about the PAP clamping down on their right to free speech and how their views are not being heard by the government—and how they're afraid of government reprisal if they express their opinions.

Yet in the recent elections, when the government allowed Singaporeans to use social media as a political tool, Singaporeans did the very things they have been criticising their government of: intimidation, and 'penalising' individuals with opposing points of view.

Furthermore in what must be the most blatant demonstration of irony ever, Singaporeans who have often complained about how biased and one-sided the local media is, then proceed to fill Facebook news feeds and Twitter timelines with strictly anti-PAP/pro-opposition articles or status updates.

But perhaps the biggest exhibition of hypocrisy must come from the Singaporeans who have been banging on about the virtues of a "true democracy" prior to the elections.

Thousands of Singaporeans then converged on a single constituency to demand a by-election because voters in that constituency voted for the PAP, albeit by a small margin of slightly more than a hundred votes.

Singapore's Political and Economic Situation

Although I may be critical of the behaviour of some Singaporeans on social media, I can also understand where they're coming from.

After all, politics is a subject that inherently stirs up emotional responses. Even rational decisions are often only rational to the particular individual and not to anyone else.

I found it extremely hard to decide who to vote for in my constituency. There was really only one party you could vote for: the PAP. The problem with every other political party in Singapore is that they tend to be merged into a single entity: the opposition. As individual parties, none of them truly stand out or have distinct ideological differences from each other.

Therefore when you enter the voting booth, you are indicating your belief on whether you think the ruling party is doing a good job, or whether you think someone else can do a better job.

The undeniable fact is that ever since the PAP came into power 48 years ago, Singapore has been a shining beacon of what a guided economy should turn out to be. Despite having little to no natural resources available in Singapore, Singapore's economy is incredibly successful owing to government intervention and guidance.

According to the [conservative U.S. think tank the] Heritage Foundation, Singapore is the 2nd freest economy in the world. Singapore is also [the] only Asian country with AAA ratings from Moody's, Standard & Poor's and Fitch Ratings. Apart from that, Singapore also has the 3rd highest GDP [gross domestic product] per capita (PPP) in the world, the 2nd highest real GDP growth rate in the world for 2010, the 3rd highest industrial production growth rate in the world, the 9th largest current account balance in the world, the 11th largest reserves of foreign exchange and gold in the world, and one of the lowest unemployment rates in the world. Despite not having a drop of crude oil on their soil, Singapore somehow is also the 18th largest exporter of oil in the world.

The undeniable fact is that ever since the PAP came into power 48 years ago, Singapore has been a shining beacon of what a guided economy should turn out to be.

However, many Singaporeans feel that the economic success we enjoy has come at a high price where unpopular policies are implemented for the sake of the economy. These unpopular policies, including the high influx of foreign workers and the increasing cost of living, have negatively affected the day-to-day lives of Singaporeans. . . .

Despite winning 81 out of 87 seats in parliament, the PAP has recognized the need to reconnect with the local population. However, based on social media sentiments, this looks to be an increasingly hard task.

Singapore is growing into a true democracy, and freedom of speech is finally here. So how will Singapore's political system and economy change in the next five years?

The Web That Failed: How Opposition Politics and Independent Initiatives Are Failing on the Internet in Russia

Floriana Fossato and John Lloyd with Alexander Verkhovsky

Floriana Fossato is a research associate at the Reuters Institute for the Study of Journalism; John Lloyd is director of journalism at the Reuters Institute; and Alexander Verkhovsky is the director of the SOVA Center for Information and Analysis. In the following viewpoint, the authors argue that the Internet has not been a force for political liberalization in Russia. Rather, they argue, the regime of Vladimir Putin has been able to use the web for propaganda purposes. They say that the regime has not used outright censorship but has instead driven the Internet conversation by recruiting bloggers, setting up official sites, and allowing occasional haphazard local crackdowns. The authors conclude that the potential of the Internet is dependent on local context and is not necessarily democratizing.

As you read, consider the following questions:

1. What different sorts of liberation do the authors say the Internet might promote?

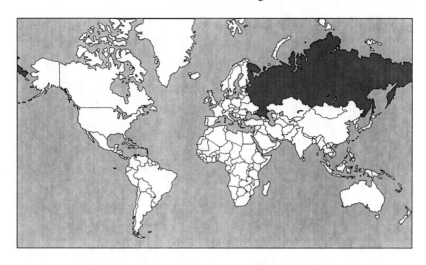

2. To what five antidemocratic Internet trends do the authors say their research has pointed?

3. What do the authors say has characterized Internet activism against the Russian war in Chechnya?

Most of the news media in Russia are now strongly pro-regime, as a matter of state policy. They are not wholly state controlled, nor have they reverted to the wooden conformity of the Soviet era. But the often chaotic liberty they enjoyed in the decade from the late 1980s to the late 1990s has been replaced by media whose diversity, curiosity and investigative capacity are tightly limited, while the leading commentators, both print and broadcast, are strongly pro-regime in most of their basic policies.

Yet as the Russian media were closing, there developed, globally, a medium which was seen as an antidote to state dominance. The Internet has come to be seen as a liberator, a tool whose possession, or ability to access, allows individuals, opposition parties and NGOs to escape the control the state can exercise over TV and radio channels, and the press. This report is a first attempt to gauge how far that is true in Russia. . . .

There are more than 300,000 noncommercial organisations identified by Russia's Public Chamber as existing and active in Russia, most of which have Internet sites: a major study of these would reveal much about civil society in Russia today. In addition, Russians can freely access foreign websites—though few of these are in Russian—and can and do take part in social sites, such as MySpace for example. But this activity is largely confined to a small group, often composed of those conversant in a foreign language, usually English. What we wish to provide is a succinct and preliminary appreciation of the nature of the Russian-produced Internet, one which could give a glimpse into the way it works, how far it reaches out to its audience and how much effect it is likely to have. . . .

The theory of the Internet as a social and political tool assumes a number of different sorts of liberation. One is liberation from state control, as bloggers—even in societies which seek to censor their output, like China—evade control and publish material the authorities wish to suppress. Another is liberation from the capture of the means of communication by large corporations—even if the limits they impose are wide, they are nevertheless limits. Still another liberation is from limited sources, as the expansion of the net's resources of information brings vast libraries of knowledge and information to domestic screens, giving each *netizen* the potential for endless enquiry, scholarship and self-improvement. Liberation is defined, above all, as a personal liberation—from the limits set by states, by corporations, by the inaccessibility of information and knowledge. Liberation is defined as serving the potential and ability of each individual, allowing the free trade of views, information and commodities.

Our initial, and most important, result indicates that the liberation promise may be limited in Russia. The why and the how of that we seek to tell and show in this essay. First, however, we should set a little context.

The Russia of the latter years of the first decade of the third millennium is one which has recovered some of the power and pride of its high Soviet period. Above all its leadership, with the support of the majority of its people, has sought with success to characterize as shameful, and to put behind it, the immediate post-Soviet period of the 1990s, the 'Yeltsin years', seeing it as a time where a weakened, ill-led and carelessly complaisant state bowed to the designs of the West—in its defence and strategic posture, in its economic policies and in its political and social organisation. Former president, now prime minister, Vladimir Putin called the collapse of the Soviet Union 'the greatest geopolitical disaster of the (20th) century'—a high claim to make of a century so rich in geopolitical disasters, including in his own country's Soviet period, but one which clearly resonates with his fellow Russians.

Our initial, and most important, result indicates that the liberation promise may be limited in Russia.

Much of that growth in confidence and assertiveness is based on very strong growth in the economy, which is putting Russia back among the stronger economies of the world. Shrinking through most of the 1990s, the Russian economy has since the early 2000s been growing at 7 per cent annually, a rate it seems likely to be able to sustain. In the eight years to 2006, the Russian economy grew by more than 50 per cent, poverty was halved and personal income grew by over 60 per cent. This relatively rapid improvement in the conditions of almost all Russians—most of whom had been fearful of their living standards, even their lives, in the economic decline of the 1990s—has meant that the administration's view of Russia, its future and itself, is widely accepted and celebrated.

For most Western observers, this change has been seen as one which may be good for the Russians' material lives, but is bad for their democratic rights—and even more, those of their neighbours. The scholar and writer Timothy Garton Ash writes that 'although formally an electoral democracy, the Russian federation has currently strong authoritarian tendencies, and is attempting to recreate a sphere of influence in Eastern Europe and the Caucasus'.[1] The geopolitical analyst Robert Kagan writes that

> Since the mid-1990s, the nascent democratic transformation in Russia has given way to what may best be described as a 'czarist' political system, in which all important decisions are taken by one man and his powerful coterie. Vladimir Putin and his coterie speak of 'democracy', but they define the term much as the Chinese do.[2]

The extent of this control of the media is not total: Edward Lucas, in a book harshly critical of the expanding authority and authoritarianism of the Russian regime and of the West for doing too little to oppose it, notes that dissident newspapers (such as *Novaya Gazeta*) can be bought, an oppositionist radio station (Ekho Moskvy) is on the air and a sometimes feisty TV station (REN TV) broadcasts—both in Moscow and in the regions. Above all, 'the Internet remains largely uncensored for any Russian with the time to browse it'.[3] But the media are controlled as much as the regime wishes: 'by 2004, Mr. Putin had the media and business under his thumb'.

This is not a portrait of North Korea—nor even of Cuba. Those who wish to live in opposition to the regime can express that opposition in a number of forms: They will not benefit by it, but nor will they, in the main, obviously suffer for it (though some of its toughest critics, as journalist Anna Politkovskaya and former KGB officer turned critic Alexander Litvinenko, have been murdered). To be sure, the people's and the government's wills have been brought into close alignment; for those who refuse such a prospect, there are other places to go. One of these places is—or, so it is widely believed, should be—the web. . . .

The media are controlled as much as the regime wishes.

Our research has pointed to the following trends, each of which would repay more detailed and extensive investigation:

- the qualitative level of Internet discussion seems to be low;

- lack of trust is widespread and on occasion skillfully manipulated by the authorities;

- online networks seem to be generally rather closed and tend to the intolerant;

- it seems that leaders of Internet sites can often be co-opted, compromised or frightened;

- Russian Internet users appear not to respond actively to political campaigning on the web. For these reasons, Russians have for some time been much less sanguine about Internet developments than . . . foreign observers. . . . Boris Dubin, a director of the Levada-Centre for sociological research, told our project[4] that

the hopes of those who expect civil society activities in Russia to increase and have a significant impact on the off-line world seem quite naïve. Since the Internet is essentially a horizontal communication network, a corresponding vertical network is needed for the creation of ideas that can translate into off-line activity and mobilisation.

Dubin's phrase would remind a Russian of the more common formula used by the Kremlin, a 'vertical of power', by which is meant a structure which reaches deep into the political and social system. His adaptation of it means, he said, a network of 'existing institutes, whose functions are sometimes obstructed, but whose existence is nonetheless respected by society and by the political leadership'.

He believes that all institutions of civil society have been emasculated and manipulated by the authorities in recent years. Thus the Internet, in his view, has been restricted to the status of 'a device to test one's own circle' and, although in a slightly different way from in the Soviet period (more technical, modern, creative), can be used to reproduce well-tested mechanisms of propaganda and manipulation.

It is, of course, the case that Internet activity and Internet engagement are increasing strongly, in Russia as elsewhere—as Dubin recognises. But though he sees this as positive, it is more than balanced, he believes, by an increase in a wide range of provocations and manipulation—a development he sees as 'poisoning' meaningful platforms for dialogue and discussion. Russia's society, he says, is essentially 'guided by simple, quite archaic frameworks—and for this reason the value of Internet and blogs for the development of civil society is extremely limited'.

Dubin's view of the limitations of the Internet to create (as against amplifying) the links, networks and habits of civil society accords with the view of social scientists who study the effects of different communications technologies, such as, for example, Robin Brown of the Leeds Institute of Communications who writes that

> mobilization is not only something that nongovernmental actors do, but something that states do. States have provided the framework within which other political actors have emerged—parties, trade unions, social movements. Yet the current wave of interest in mobilization and new technologies is driven by the belief that new developments are breaking down this pattern and driving a shift of power away from the state.[5]

In Russia, however, the state has strengthened itself over the period of office of President Vladimir Putin, and does not seem to be about to allow a shift of power away soon. The power and potential of the Russian Internet is severely limited. From our research, and from intense monitoring of a selected number of websites and blogs of individuals and organisations, we argue that, in the Russian context, at present at least, new communications developments are not yet breaking down well-established patterns of power. The state remains the main mobilising agent in Russia. Following a few years of spontaneous—and inexpensive—'anarchy', Ruet currently does operate as a device to spread information, but largely among closed clusters of like-minded users who are seldom able or willing to cooperate. However, it does operate as a platform which the state uses increasingly successfully to consolidate its power and spread messages of stability and unity among the growing number of Russians regularly accessing websites and blogs.

In the Russian context, at present at least, new communications developments are not yet breaking down well-established patterns of power.

A paper by Markku Lonkila on 'The Internet and Anti-Military Activism in Russia'[6] reveals that the movement against the war in Chechnya, whose main activists are the mothers of soldiers serving there, is split into different, sometimes hostile, factions; has little or no links with antiwar movements elsewhere; and limits its protests exclusively to Chechnya, and largely to the soldiers' conditions. Lonkila finds that the net antiwar movement lacks coherence—but adds that this is in line with the fragmentation of off-line forms of activism, an underscoring of the point that the net cannot and does not bestow any new element not already there in the activists' behaviour. His study, Lonkila concludes, 'suggests that the online anti-military activism on the Russian Internet is fragmented and run by a small group of activists'.

Those in the Kremlin supporting a 'third way', a soft approach to the management of the 'vertical of power' built by President Vladimir Putin have clearly prevailed so far in the matter of managing the Internet, and the opinions expressed on it. Selective and well-publicised cases of outspoken, oppositionist websites and blogs which have been closed down by the authorities in a number of regions are more the overzealous initiative of local authorities than a planned move from the centre—for all that these sporadic crackdowns may be welcomed in Moscow, because of the feeling of fear and suspended punishment that they spread among Internet users. We have noted that President Medvedev has taken a relatively liberal line in regard to proposed legislation to control the Internet: It is too soon to judge if this will remain a settled policy.

Such cases, however, have been the exception rather than the norm in Russia at this time. The advantage of widespread, increasingly skillful and creative manipulation has been twofold. In the first place it is manipulation, not censorship, that effectively defuses the attraction of political activity among the young population—the more so since entertainment is used as a weapon. As the British scholar Andrew Wilson put it in a recent interview with RFE/RL, 'In the society of the spectacle, your spectacle has to be spectacular.' In the second place, by avoiding the overt Internet censorship that the Chinese authorities enforce, the Kremlin has placed itself in an advantageous position *vis-à-vis* those in the West who routinely demand freedom of expression in Russia. The new president, Dmitry Medvedev, has said in interviews that he is an avid Internet user and is fully satisfied by the degree of diversity of opinions on offer on the Russian segment of the Internet.

We were lucky to have completed our project during the first part of the Russian electoral cycle. We recorded a wealth of information on pro-Kremlin Internet manipulation, including 'brigades' of bloggers which spread the president's message online and which took great pleasure in disrupting the online activities of Kremlin opponents, by using abusive language and obstructing discussions, or acting in an organised way to prevent certain issues making the headlines on the influential Yandex Top 20 issues of the day.

Our monitoring confirmed the amplitude of the manipulation effort, although it was not at the centre of the present research. One of the main names who emerged was 28-year-old Konstantin Rykov (whose LiveJournal was formerly <http://real-rykov.livejournal.com>; the journal was deleted and purged during our monitoring) who became a member of the State Duma on the United Russia party list in the Nizhny Novgorod region in December 2007. Rykov has been the editor in chief of Kremlin-friendly online newspaper *Vzglyad* <http://www.vzglyad.ru> that is one of the 10 most visited news sites in Russian, according to Rambler statistics <http://top100.rambler.ru/top100/Media/index.shtml.ru>.

It is manipulation, not censorship, that effectively defuses the attraction of political activity among the young population—the more so since entertainment is used as a weapon.

Rykov has also been identified by Russian media as one of the creators of the website <Zaputina.ru> that was launched in November 2007. <Gazeta.ru> said on 9 November that 'the distinctive feature of the parliamentary election has been the use of Internet technologies. Political technologists in the United Russia camp make ample use of these technologies.'[7]

The logos of both these projects are aimed at recalling the logo style of the Rossiya state television channel—thus providing a direct link between the channel and the regime's propaganda output. There are only three sections on the websites—politics, society and music—and during the campaign, the politics section was entirely structured around carefully produced propagandistic video spots. One video clip on <Zaputina.ru> is borrowed from Rossiya television: It was named 'The Day of the Jackal' and covers the 'Dissenters' March' of 24 November.

In the clip, Mahler's first symphony is used as the musical background to fragments of Putin's electoral speech in front of 'United Russia' activists at Luzhniki Stadium on 21 November. The picture is framed to correspond perfectly to the president's words. When Putin says 'unfortunately there are still in our country those who scrounge from foreign embassies like jackals', the picture on the screen is synchronised to show Kasparov. When Putin talks about 'those who in the 1990s during their tenure in office caused huge damage to society and to the state as they served the needs of oligarchs', the picture is that of Boris Nemtsov, who in 1998, at the time of the financial crisis, was serving as deputy prime minister. And when Putin declares that 'they are responsible for making corruption the main mean of economic competition', the picture moves to Maria Gaidar, daughter of Yegor Gaidar, the architect of Russia's economic reform.

The launch of these websites during the parliamentary campaign was aimed at involving as many young people as possible in the electoral process. Several Internet experts commented to <Gazeta.ru> that it would be impossible to measure the effectiveness of these activities. Anton Nosik of SUP told <Gazeta.ru> that the emergence of propagandist websites of this kind makes use of budgets allocated to support Kremlin-friendly political propaganda. . . .

We agree very largely with the conclusions of Rafal Rohozinski, a British-based scholar who served as adviser on 'digital divide' issues to the United Nations. In a 1999 report that examined the emergence of new telecommunication technologies in the late years of the Soviet Union and in the early post-Soviet era[8] Rohozinski said that the Russian case vividly shows to what extent 'the impact of information technologies is critically shaped by the social context in which they are deployed. . . . Thus, what is the most interesting about the Internet's emergence in Russia is not the way in which technology transformed society, but rather the way in which society colonised the technology."[9]

There is no shortcut for which the code is www.

We do not question the notion that the growth in accessible telecommunication technologies can advance democracy and freedom, modifying the power relation between individuals, groups and governments. However, we agree with Rohozinski who says that 'the leap to declaring that these technologies also have the ability to reinforce, or even create, democracies, is a long one indeed'.

What we witness here is a clash of quite differing views on the 'promise' of the Internet. For liberals, that promise—as we defined it above—is of various kinds of individual liberation. For those in power in Russia—and it seems for a majority of the Russian people—the promise is nothing like so clear-cut. Though they may, and do, attest to its usefulness, it is also suspect for a different kind of potential: not just for individual liberation, but for social manipulation. The necessity, strongly proposed by the government and at least passively assented to by the majority, for a nation at one with itself, militates against an active net culture. The medium does not carry the inevitable message of individual liberation. It depends upon larger messages, actions and traditions. There is no shortcut for which the code is www.

Notes

1. Timothy Garton Ash, *Free World: How a Crisis of the West Reveals the Opportunity of Our Time* (London: Penguin, 2004), 213.
2. Robert Kagan, *The Return of History* (London: Atlantic Books, 2008).
3. Edward Lucas, *The New Cold War* (London: Bloomsbury, 2008), 55–6.
4. Interview with Boris Dublin (Sept. 2007).

5. Robin Brown, 'Mobilizing the Bias of Communication: Information Technology, Political Communications and Transitional Political Strategy', paper for panel of the American Political Science Association Convention, Washington DC (Aug.-Sept. 2000).
6. *Europe-Asia Studies*, 60/7 (Sept. 2006).
7. http://www.gazeta.ru/politics/elections2007/articles/2296913.shtml.
8. Rafal Rohozinski, *Mapping Russian Cyberspace: A Perspective on Democracy and the Net* (Geneva: UNRISD, 1999), <http://www.unrisd.org/infotech/confern/russian/toc.htm>.
9. The UNRISD report was the basis for an article in *Current History* (Oct. 2000), <http://www.cdi.org/russia/johnson/5014.html##7>.

Periodical and Internet Sources Bibliography

The following articles have been selected to supplement the diverse views presented in this chapter.

Peter Beaumont	"The Truth About Twitter, Facebook and the Uprisings in the Arab World," *Guardian*, February 24, 2011.
Irina Borogan and Andrei Soldatov	"The Kremlin Versus the Bloggers: The Battle for Cyberspace," openDemocracy, March 27, 2012. www.opendemocracy.net.
Torie Bosch	"Tangled Web," *Slate*, February 1, 2011. www.slate.com.
Shadi Bushra	"Democracy's Domino Effect: Protests in Sudan," *Stanford Progressive*, January 2011.
Economist	"Social Networks: Facebook and Freedom," September 29, 2010.
John Hudson	"The 'Twitter Revolution' Debate: The Egyptian Test Case," The Atlantic Wire, January 31, 2011. www.theatlanticwire.com.
David Lundquist	"Can China Control Social Media?," The Diplomat, January 19, 2012. http://the-diplomat.com.
Evgeny Morozov	"Iran Elections: A Twitter Revolution?," *Washington Post*, June 17, 2009.
Dana Radcliffe	"Can Social Media Undermine Democracy?," *Huffington Post*, October 18, 2011. www.huffingtonpost.com.
Andrew Sullivan	"Could Tunisia Be the Next Twitter Revolution?," *Daily Dish*, January 13, 2011. www.theatlantic.com.

GLOBALVIEWPOINTS

CHAPTER 4

Social Networking and Access to Information

Social Media Privacy Issues Must Be Addressed

David Lindsay and Ian Brown, as told to Damien Carrick

David Lindsay is a professor of law at Monash University; Ian Brown is codirector of the information and security program at the Oxford Internet Institute; and Damien Carrick is a lawyer and a law reporter for the Australian Broadcasting Corporation's Radio National. In the following viewpoint, the authors discuss the issue of privacy and freedom of information. They highlight cases in which information placed online through social networks has been used against individuals. They also offer instances in which information released anonymously has been traced back to individuals. They conclude that the public needs to be better informed, and that governments and other organizations need to do a better job of controlling information.

As you read, consider the following questions:

1. Who is Stacy Snyder, and what privacy issues did she face, according to David Lindsay?
2. What law does Ian Brown say Germany is passing to address issues of privacy on social networks?
3. What is one example Ian Brown presents of cases in which supposedly anonymous data was traced back to individuals?

Damien Carrick: Professor David Lindsay is based at Monash University. He was one of the organisers of a conference held in Melbourne last week [in February 2012] looking at emerging challenges in privacy law. He thinks we need to look closely at how we regulate the digital footprint we leave on social media, because all too often we don't put our best foot forward.

Photos Used Against You

David Lindsay: Stacy Snyder is a single mother, she was enrolled in a teaching degree in the United States and back in 2006 she posted to her MySpace site a photograph of herself wearing a pirate's hat, a very innocuous photo, a pirate's hat with a glass and captioned it 'drunken pirate'. As a result of that, she was refused permission to graduate from her teaching degree, and then she launched an action against the college and was unsuccessful in that action, and consequently she has really become a poster child for problems relating to information that has been posted to a social networking site in one context and then comes back to bite you when it's used in a completely different, unexpected context.

And tell me, David Lindsay, I understand even your own students often tell you about their experiences.

Lindsay: The most common experiences, when a friend of theirs has posted a photograph to a social networking site and they ask their friend to take down that photograph, and the problems that they usually have is that when a friend decides that they don't want to take down that information. The problem is this, is the different interests that relate to the digital information, because one person has an interest in having photographs of himself with his friends, or herself with her friends, another person objects to that. How do you balance these interests of the different people that are, whose personal information is made public? This really highlights the essential problem of social networking, is that it straddles and blurs distinctions between what off-line is considered to be a private interaction, considered not to be public, and what becomes public, because once information is digital it persists over time, it's something we call digital eternity, and it flows, and it's copied, and it's duplicated. And because of that, it can then come back to haunt or perhaps imprison people in their digital pasts.

But in the absence of a cultural sea change, we have to rely on the law, and it seems most research suggests young people don't have a realistic handle on how online information can be used. Doctor Ian Brown is from the Oxford Internet Institute.

Ian Brown: There was one study done in the United States where a large number of college-aged students were asked five straightforward questions about their privacy rights, and actually over 40 per cent of those students got all the questions wrong. They were so confused, they thought they actually had a lot more protection in American law than they really do have.

The essential problem of social networking is that it straddles and blurs distinctions between what off-line is considered to be a private interaction . . . and what becomes public.

What sorts of questions were they asked?

Brown: If something they thought they'd shared with a limited number of people became more widely available, what rights did they have to stop information that they'd shared being used in a negative way against them. They really did seem to think that the law gave them all sorts of rights that in reality, particularly in the US, which doesn't have omnibus privacy law, which they don't have.

I guess, though, one of the common scenarios is that a prospective employer finds a compromising or inappropriate photo on Facebook, whether or not they can use that in their selection process.

Brown: Absolutely, and Germany is one of the few countries that's really explicitly now addressing this question where there's been a lot of public disquiet, and the German government is legislating to say employers must not use private online spaces such as Facebook.

That's going to become a law in Germany, and that sounds like it's one of the first jurisdictions to actually bring in this kind of regulation.

Brown: That's right, and I think what else is interesting in that discussion is broadening the protections for privacy out from specific privacy laws as exist in Australia, in Europe, to other areas like employment law, like general antidiscrimination law.

Privacy and Free Information

Of course, there's always a tension between the right to privacy and the general well-being that we all derive from having the free flow of information. Ian Brown says regulators in the UK [United Kingdom] have had to deal with a number of disputes where what appears to be anonymised statistical information might be able to identify individuals.

Brown: They've had interesting cases in the past where they've had to decide . . . one party's asking the government to release a particular set of records, for example statistics on the number of leukaemia cases, which the government agency concerned is concerned that releasing that data will infringe on people's privacy.

How?

Brown: The concern has been that if you release data about something that's quite unusual, like leukaemia cases in a specific region, for example, you might start to allow people to combine that with other information and find the actual individuals you're talking about. The latest development here comes from UK government plans for government to be much more open with the data that it holds, to by default think

Facebook and Beacon

Some social networking sites have gotten into trouble when they take actions that violate user expectations about making information public. One of the most notorious examples of this in the social networking arena is the Facebook advertising program called "Beacon." Facebook launched Beacon in November 2007. The program connected Facebook users' activities on outside websites to the users' Facebook news feed. The Beacon ad program launched with 44 external partner websites, including Yelp, eBay, and Fandango. At its inception, Facebook users were automatically opted in for Beacon, and any user who wanted to opt out of Beacon had to learn about it and then take action. Famously, a Facebook user bought a diamond ring at a partner site as a Christmas gift for his wife. The purchase was meant to be a surprise, but it was broadcast on his Facebook news feed, where his wife and all his Facebook friends saw it. Later, Facebook changed the Beacon program to require a participant to affirmatively opt in and provided a tool to allow users to turn off the program entirely. After a class action lawsuit, Facebook abandoned the program altogether.

Robert Gellman and Pam Dixon,
Online Privacy: A Reference Handbook.
Santa Barbara, CA: ABC-CLIO, 2011, p. 45.

about publishing data sets both that aren't related to individuals, so things like the location of bus stops or weather data, but more recently also data like health records or education records.

As I understand it, there's been a lot of release of government information around crime in particular areas, and that has also been quite controversial. Why?

Brown: One of the first stages of this open data program with data that touched on individuals was the release of crime mapping statistics by the UK government. What those showed were the number of instances of crimes and antisocial behaviour in very specific geographic areas. So, for privacy reasons, that data was not down to the individual household, but perhaps to a group of streets, you could see that there'd been maybe three burglaries in the last year. There was a lot of interest in that, people were fascinated to see what was going on in their neighbourhood. There were some people that had concerns; well if the data gets too specific, it might allow somebody to figure out, well it was you that was burgled, and actually that's a sign to criminals that your house is an easy touch, and they might come back the following month.

The concern has been that if you release data about something that's quite unusual, like leukaemia cases in a specific region . . . you might start to allow people to . . . find the actual individuals you're talking about.

Walk me through how people might use what is to my ears anonymised information—the number of people with a particular illness in a particular area or the number of burglaries in a particular area—walk me through how somebody might connect the dots and identify me.

Brown: So, I'll give you two examples of cases that happened in the United States with what seemed like quite innocuous data but then was re-identified to individuals. So, AOL the search engine several years ago decided they would publish lists of anonymised search queries that they had answered, an enterprising journalist at the *New York Times* decided, 'Well if I look through these lists of search queries, maybe I can start to link some of them together, and especially if people were searching for information about themselves or about their neighbourhood, work out who the people were behind the search queries.' And actually the *New York Times* journalist ended up knocking on the door of somebody and saying, 'Is this you?' and it was, and the person was really amazed and then slightly shocked that AOL had released this data and enabled this process.

The other more recent example was when the US company Netflix decided they wanted to improve their movie recommendation algorithm, so they thought, 'Well, why don't we publish a big list of all of the movie rentals of our customers, anonymised, so we'll take off identifying details, then we offer a prize for somebody that can make a better recommender algorithm.' What then happened, though, was some computer science researchers thought, 'Well, we have this other database of people's movie interests over here called IMDb', which is a free website that lets people file movie reviews, and it turned out that it was actually very easy to correlate the Netflix set of data. You could see that certain individuals in the Netflix database had borrowed certain movies and there were corresponding reviews, sets of reviews, on IMDb, and often user names that actually made it very obvious who the person was. And so suddenly somebody that had borrowed a wide range of movies on Netflix maybe reviewed four or five of them on IMDb, that allowed their whole rental history to be traced, and there might be some movies on there about controversial topics that they were not happy for that to be linked back to them in person.

Governments are going to have to say we are going to keep the data ourselves under tight control.

Data Control

So what's the best way forward here? What lessons are there here for regulators, or the way we go about organising ourselves? So we allow for the research, we allow for the transparent use of as much information as we can, because there are really good benefits from doing so, but on the other hand protecting people's privacy?

Brown: So absolutely, you can see that there could be great social benefits. To do that, governments are going to have to say we are going to keep the data ourselves under tight control, we will allow researchers to come and make use of that data to analyse it, you know, in our facilities or perhaps in tightly controlled facilities, but we're not going to put it out into the world; it's just too sensitive for that. There might be other data where there is effective anonymisation processes the government can go through that will reduce the risk to a low enough level the data can just be literally put on a website and made available to anyone who's interested.

The German Government Is Demanding That Facebook Address Privacy Concerns

Christopher Williams

Christopher Williams is technology correspondent for the Telegraph. In the following viewpoint, he reports that Facebook is facing serious privacy concerns and government regulation in Germany. In the United States, Williams says, Facebook compromised by allowing users to have more control of their data. German regulators, however, have been harsher, and have even in some cases demanded the removal of Facebook's "Like" button. Williams says that Germany has a very strong tradition of privacy law, linked in part to East Germany's terrible experiences with the Communist secret police.

As you read, consider the following questions:

1. According to Williams, what concessions did Facebook make to avoid all-out war with the US government?

2. Why does Williams say that Hamburg's data protection authority is preparing court action against Facebook?

3. Why does Williams say that it is not surprising that Facebook and Germany are fighting on the front line of privacy in the digital age?

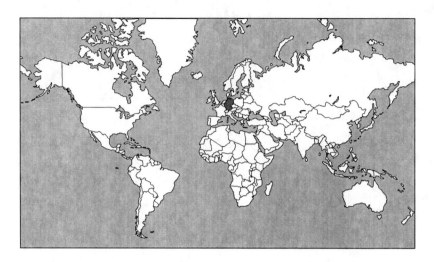

Facebook is engaged in battles with privacy watchdogs all over the world. This week [in December 2011], it signalled a truce on home territory when Mark Zuckerberg [cofounder of Facebook] admitted a "bunch of mistakes" on the issue and pledged a series of policy changes to satisfy American regulators.

Compromise with the United States

The mea culpa [admitted error] was prompted by an investigation by the Federal Trade Commission, which accused Facebook of "unfair and deceptive" practices that invaded its users' privacy. The world's dominant social network "deceived consumers by telling them they could keep their information on Facebook private, and then repeatedly allowing it to be shared and made public", it charged.

By agreeing to get permission from users before exposing more of their data, and allowing external audits of his privacy systems, Mr Zuckerberg has ceded enough ground to avoid all-out war with the United States government ahead of Facebook's $100bn [billion] public listing, expected next year [in 2012].

On the German front, however, entente is proving more difficult. Europe's economic powerhouse, home to more than 20 million Facebook users, has no fewer than 17 official bodies responsible for enforcing data protection and privacy laws; one federal and one for each of the 16 states.

Some of them see Facebook as the web's chief privacy villain and some of its features as examples of an American company ignoring European laws. Privacy laws in EU [European Union] countries, including Britain, have to at least meet standards set by officials in Brussels. British regulators have demurred in response to privacy trangressions by the giants of the web, such as when Google's Street View cars intercepted WiFi data. That is not the case throughout the EU, however.

Most recently, Hamburg's data protection authority, a regional equivalent of Britain's Information Commissioner, said it was preparing court action against Facebook over its introduction of facial recognition technology earlier this year. The "Tag Suggestions" feature tries to automatically identify and "tag" friends who appear in users' photos. It was rolled out in Europe over the summer with scant warning.

On the German front, however, entente is proving more difficult.

"Unequivocal consent of the parties is required by both European and national data protection law," the Hamburg authority charged, adding that "further negotiations are pointless". The Teutonic [Germanic] bluntness was a sign of the mutual frustration that characterises Facebook's dealings with German regulators.

In another ongoing case, the privacy regulator for the northern state of Schleswig-Holstein has taken issue with Facebook's ubiquitous "Like" button. It allows users to share

On Facebook, 273 people know I'm a dog.
The rest can only see my limited profile.

links with their Facebook friends by simply clicking on a thumbs-up icon on third-party websites. Because of the way the button collects data on those users, websites in the region are in the process of removing it from all their pages, on the orders of the regional privacy regulator, Thilo Weichert.

"Many Facebook offerings are in conflict with the law," he said. "This unfortunately has not prevented website owners from using the respective services and the more so as they are easy to install and free of charge."

"Like" Wars

His interpretation of the facts has caused special exasperation at Facebook, which argues that by not allowing websites to include elements such as the "Like" button, Mr Weichert has effectively decided to "break the web".

"The technology used by the Like button, known as an 'iFrame', is in common usage across the web and is valued by many website owners as it offers them a simple way to make their sites more useful to people," said spokeswoman Tina Kulow, referring to the way modern web pages typically include content that they do not serve up themselves. For example, a newspaper website might include a box containing, say, live football scores, which is actually published by a third party.

"As well as the Like button, the same technology is used for embedding other forms of content on websites such as videos, maps and advertisements," she said.

"We believe that this technology can be deployed in a privacy-friendly way and have taken great care to put in place appropriate protections for our use of the technology."

Although Facebook maintains an impeccable corporate manner in its public dealings with German regulators, in private the frustration is palpable. Executives believe that some officials do not understand the technology they seek to restrict and play to the gallery rather than address the issues constructively.

That the front line of privacy in the digital age should be fought by Facebook and Germany is hardly surprising. On one side stands Mark Zuckerberg with the stated aim of breaking down privacy barriers and provoking the world to share more. On the other stands a nation with more reason than any other to fear intrusion by powerful organisations; the tyranny of the Stasi [the East German Communist secret police] is easily within living memory.

According to Professor Douwe Korff, an expert in data protection and international law at London Metropolitan University, "privacy is very deeply embedded in German law".

Although Facebook maintains an impeccable corporate manner in its public dealings with German regulators, in private the frustration is palpable.

"They have very strong constitutional protection of privacy rights and the data protection authorities are much more forceful than the Information Commissioner, and the people I have worked with there are very tech-savvy," he said.

"I think there is just a lack of understanding on both sides; it would be better if they could just work together to get the right policies and technology in place to protect privacy."

"I think this is going to be a very important test case to decide how companies behave towards individual privacy online. The public are increasingly aware of the issue."

Mark Zuckerberg has made all the right noises this week, promising to make Facebook the "leader in transparency and control around privacy", admitting it could "always do better" and pledging to embrace regulation. In Germany he still has many critics to convince, however.

Britain's Internet Crackdown Could Herald More Censorship of the Internet

Peter Apps

Peter Apps is a politics and economics correspondent for Reuters. In the following viewpoint, he reports that British prime minister David Cameron has discussed censoring social media sites after widespread riots in the United Kingdom during 2011. Apps says that Cameron's discussion of censorship has been greeted with approval in China, where the government has long been criticized for its tight censorship of the Internet. On the other hand, Apps says, many Western commentators have been concerned that Cameron's move might lead to wider Western censorship, which would be antidemocratic and damaging to globalization.

As you read, consider the following questions:

1. According to Apps, what techniques has China used to control Internet access?
2. In what way might limiting access to social media sites to curb social unrest backfire, according to Apps?

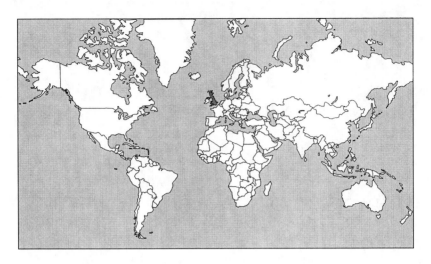

3. What does Heather Brooke say could happen if the Internet is controlled?

British prime minister David Cameron's flirtation with the idea of social media censorship controls after recent riots [in 2011] might only be the beginning.

With Western democracies and emerging authoritarian states alike facing new threats from the rise of the Internet and social media, the temptation to try and regain control through censorship may grow.

Some experts say such attempts could backfire and jeopardise the legitimacy of governments, fuel fresh unrest and make it harder to gather intelligence and information.

Undermining Authority

One thing is certain, however. The information revolution has undermined those in authority and empowered a host of groups and individuals. Whether they are taking to the streets in large numbers to overthrow Arab leaders, organizing "flash mobs" [groups organised to meet in a given place via social media sites] to loot stores or simply spreading dissent and awkward secrets, that is changing the global balance of power.

As governments draw up strategies for cyberspace, worrying not just about crime and politics but also the risk of militant or military attacks on critical infrastructure, they face fundamental questions about the power and limits of the state.

"One of the biggest challenges . . . is on the conceptual level," says John Bassett, a former senior official at Britain's signals intelligence agency GCHQ [Government Communications Headquarters] and now a senior fellow at London's Royal United Services Institute.

"Does a government attempt to control cyberspace as it would have tried to control its (real world) borders in the 20th century or does it develop security doctrines that go beyond traditional models of state control?"

Whilst China in particular has tried to control Internet access through its "great firewall" and a sophisticated network of censors, filters and internal monitoring, most states have embraced a largely unfettered, globalised Internet.

But despite Western rhetoric on free speech and criticism of authoritarian states for attempts to limit it—for example, of [former Egyptian president] Hosni Mubarak's abortive attempt to shut down Egypt's Internet—the reality has always been more complex.

"Does a government attempt to control cyberspace as it would have tried to control its (real world) borders in the 20th century?"

Attempts by the United States and its allies to block the dissemination of leaked State Department cables via WikiLeaks might have largely failed, but Julian Assange [the head of WikiLeaks] and his organization have been left largely starved of funds.

Agencies such as Britain's GCHQ and the U.S. National Security Agency have huge powers and capabilities to monitor communications and detect crime and militancy. But trying to control what people say is another matter.

China Eyes Cameron Controls

With Cameron threatening to temporarily block social networking sites during unrest and courts imposing harsh sentences on those accused of inciting riots, Chinese authorities have detected a kindred spirit from an unexpected quarter.

"The open discussion of containment of the Internet in Britain has given rise to new opportunity for the whole world," said China's *People's Daily*, seen as a mouthpiece for the Communist Party, in a weekend editorial.

"Media in the U.S. and Britain used to criticize developing countries for curbing freedom of speech. Britain's new attitude will help appease the quarrels between East and West over the management of the Internet," it said.

Not everyone is so sure. Cameron's suggested social media controls have prompted a barrage of criticism and the sentencing of two young men to four years in prison for attempting to incite riots on Facebook was seen by some as an overreaction.

Perceptions that rioters are being given overly harsh sentences have also increased strains within the ruling Conservative–Liberal Democrat coalition.

In many states, the economic crisis is already seen as fuelling unrest amongst a younger generation whose opportunities now fall well short of their aspirations. Trying to limit their Internet and social media freedoms might only make matters worse, just as Egypt's Internet shutdown only brought more people into the streets.

With even China's microbloggers increasingly finding ways around controls to discuss online issues such as the Arab uprisings and the recent crash of a bullet train, some doubt the authorities have enough censors to keep ahead of the crowd.

"The starting point is to accept that by and large the Internet would be open and accessible whatever you try and do," John Reid, a former British defense and interior minister now running a think tank at University College London who is working on a "cyber doctrine" for Britain, told Reuters earlier this year.

"Because this technology empowers the individual, controlling it is particularly difficult to do. If you are from a censorship/control point of view, it won't work."

Challenge to Globalisation?

Some Western observers say they are appalled at Britain's suggested crackdown, saying it misses the point: In previous generations some leaders blamed dissent on the printing press, telegraph and other communications tools, and ignored underlying issues.

"Unable to identify, let alone deal with, any potential root causes of the England riots, the full weight of the political class seems to be poised to challenge what in effect is the greatest expansion of free speech and personal liberty since the rise of the personal automobile and . . . home telephones," said Alexander Klimburg, a cybersecurity expert at the Austrian Institute for International Affairs.

"This is wrong and the hysterical response will only seek to undermine confidence further in the powers that be."

"The starting point is to accept that by and large the Internet would be open and accessible whatever you try and do."

Nevertheless, many experts predict more confrontation between governments of all hues and the rising powers of the Internet, be they individual bloggers and hackers or the giant multinationals that actually control much of the traffic.

Already, Google in particular has had high-profile disputes with authorities in China, Egypt and elsewhere. In June, executive chairman Eric Schmidt said he expected such tussles to get worse.

"I suspect this is going to become a point of tension between states and corporations . . . and, more importantly, a challenge to globalization," Ian Bremmer, president of political risk consultancy Eurasia Group, wrote earlier this year.

Many experts predict more confrontation between governments of all hues and the rising powers of the Internet.

He said he believed authoritarian states in particular would try to find ways to fragment the market.

Heather Brooke, an American information campaigner living in London who was at the heart of the WikiLeaks saga, believes what she calls the "Information War" is only just beginning.

Technological advances have made it much harder for those in authority to control events and conceal secrets—such as Britain's parliamentary expenses and phone hacking scandals—but that has prompted an almost inevitable fight back.

"Power is changing," she says in an online video to publicise her new book *The Revolution Will Be Digitised.*

"The stakes are high . . . if the Internet is controlled, it could usher in an age of censorship, surveillance and oppression. Alternatively, we could be on the cusp of a new form of global democracy, with people in power."

In Mexico, Criminal Gangs Police Social Media

Samuel Logan

Samuel Logan is an investigative journalist, the director of the security consultancy agency Southern Pulse, and the author of This Is for the Mara Salvatrucha: Inside the MS-13, America's Most Violent Gang. In the following viewpoint, he reports that Mexican crime organizations have successfully targeted and murdered anonymous online users. Logan says Mexican gangs have forced hackers to aid them in targeting users. He reports that the gangs also use social media to spread messages and to commit crimes. Logan says that the Mexican government does not fully understand communication via the Internet and is ill-equipped to stop the exploitation of social media by criminals.

As you read, consider the following questions:

1. What is *Blog del Narco*, and why does it say it was started?

2. According to Logan, what is virtual extortion, and how is it facilitated by social media?

3. Logan reports on two individuals who were arrested by the Mexican government for tweeting. What does he say they had done?

Samuel Logan, "Mexico: Death by Social Media," International Relations and Security Network, September 28, 2011. Copyright © 2011 by International Relations and Security Network. All rights reserved. Reproduced by permission.

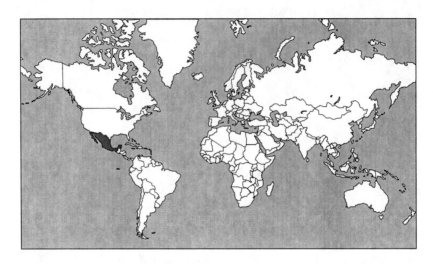

Two swinging bodies hanging from a bridge greeted commuters in Mexico's northern city of Nuevo Laredo in mid-September [2011]. The sight, sadly, was normal; the reason behind their torture and murder, however, was not. The killers—who, in the message they left, warned that "this is what will happen to all Internet busy bodies"—allegedly kidnapped and murdered the couple for comments they had posted on a popular blog focused on organized crime in Mexico. Their death will not stop anonymous readers from commenting on blog posts, but it has taken Mexico's online community by surprise—and into uncharted territory.

Crowd-Sourcing Information

In an age where Internet penetration figures have never been higher and privatized telecommunication networks allow an unprecedented number of individuals to mobilize online, social media has exploded across the world; Latin America is no exception. In Mexico, the influence of criminal organizations over traditional media networks has arguably accelerated the use of social media to report on violence in that country.

Twitter hash marks such as *#mexicorojo* have become a gateway to a torrent of information reported by people on the ground all over the country. Blogs such as *Blog del Narco, Borderland Beat, Juarez en la Sombra* and others aggregate information, photos, and videos—some of them so macabre that they could have been posted by the murderers themselves. The most popular and controversial blog, *Blog del Narco*, claims to have been started because "the media and government in Mexico try to pretend that nothing is happening, because the media is intimidated and the government has apparently been bought."

In Mexico, the influence of criminal organizations over traditional media networks has arguably accelerated the use of social media to report on violence in that country.

Elsewhere, crowd-sourced crime maps have surfaced, where users log in and report crimes in their neighborhood. The Mexican daily, *El Universal*, maintains a crowd-sourced crime map for Mexico City. A separate project has initiated a mapping system for several cities around Mexico, focusing on key variables, such as the location of criminal lookouts in their city, retail drug sales points, or where remains have been found. There is also a downloadable application for mobile devices which is used to report on corruption in Mexico City: It allows drivers to report where and when a traffic officer extorted money for a bogus traffic violation.

This shocking event has opened the door to a wide spectrum of new fears for consumers and suppliers of online media in Mexico: The rest of the message found in mid-September with the dead social media users read, "You better [expletive] pay attention. I'm about to get you."

With apparent proof that even individuals who post anonymously can be targeted with deadly reprisals, earlier concerns that criminal organizations are forcibly recruiting hackers now weigh all the more heavily.

Social Media vs. the Drug Cartels

As a consequence of the battle to control information [in the conflict between Mexico and the drug cartels], journalists, the public, and the cartels themselves have embraced "new media" technologies (i.e., social networking sites, Twitter, blogs, and other forms of horizontal self-communication). According to *Latin America News Dispatch*, "people have been using blogs and Twitter accounts to cover what many of Mexico's mainstream media outlets will not. *Blog del Narco* is one of the most notable of these outlets. According to its administrator, it receives four million visitors a week." . . .

According to the Knight Center [for Journalism in the Americas], a reaction to official news control or manipulation has stimulated cartel info ops: "A recent twist on this tight control has been the emergence of organized crime groups trying—successfully—to dictate the news agenda and impose restrictions that reaches the public." This narco-info includes intimidation and pressure: "These threats come in public statements, as well as via social networks, Internet chat rooms, e-mail, and their own news releases." As we have seen, some of this interference and pressure has led to complete or partial news blackouts in Mexico's contested regions. In areas subject to blackouts, social media and information communications technology (ICT) appear to be filling the vacuum. Again from the Knight Center, "Before the foreign press revealed what was happening in Tamaulipas, the media blackout was broken by residents of the affected towns. Armed with video cameras and cell phones, they filmed the drug smugglers' roadside checkpoints, hundreds of bullet shells on the ground after shootouts, and shoes strewn in the streets, which raised the question of what happened to their owners."

John P. Sullivan
"Attacks on Journalists and 'New Media' in Mexico's Drug War:
A Power and Counter Power Assessment,"
Small Wars Journal, April 9, 2011, pp. 13–14.

The Dark Side of Social Media

Even before this latest attack on Mexico's online community, users were under threat from criminals who used platforms such as Facebook to identify potential targets for kidnapping or, more simply, *virtual extortion*—a tactic of tricking parents into thinking that their children have been kidnapped. To fool parents, criminals trawl social media sites like MySpace and Facebook for unsecured pages that contain private, sensitive information.

Criminal groups such as Los Zetas and the Sinaloa Federation have made deft use of social media.

Though most *internautas*, as Internet surfers are called in Mexico, will be undeterred, Mexico's criminal organizations have reached an unprecedented level of online sophistication, hunting for victims and targeting specific users who post the wrong information at the wrong time. Forced to find new ways to spread fear, communicate with the rest of the world, and control their public image, criminal organizations are increasingly making use of social media tactics.

As media consumers in Mexico have seen, criminal groups such as Los Zetas and the Sinaloa Federation have made deft use of social media to send messages to their rivals, publicize their presence in a new piece of territory, or, simply, to terrorize.

Perhaps the most disturbing part of this whole trend is the recent arrest of two individuals—one a math teacher—who had tweeted information the Mexican government deemed to be sabotage and 'of a terrorist nature.' In an apparently innocent attempt to alert parents and nearby residents, the two allegedly posted that local schools in Veracruz were under attack. Though the two Twitter users have been released, the Mexican government's knee-jerk reaction speaks volumes about how little elected leaders understand the importance of social media in a country where criminals and citizens alike rely on it as an essential platform for communication.

India Is Contemplating Censoring Social Media

Sujoy Dhar

Sujoy Dhar is a correspondent for the Washington Times *and a writer for* Inter Press Service. *In the following viewpoint, he reports that an Indian government minister was slapped in public, resulting in widespread mockery on social media. Partially in response, India has been looking into censoring Internet and social media content that it deems offensive to religious sentiments. Critics say that the move is an effort to limit criticism of the government and government corruption. Dhar maintains that experts say it would be extremely difficult to censor the Internet in line with the Indian government's requests.*

As you read, consider the following questions:

1. What is "Why This Kolaveri Di?," and how was it used to embarrass the Indian government?

2. Who is Gaurav Bakshi, and to what does he attribute the Indian government's interest in censoring the Internet?

3. Who is Divyanshu Dutta Roy, and what does he say makes the web wonderful?

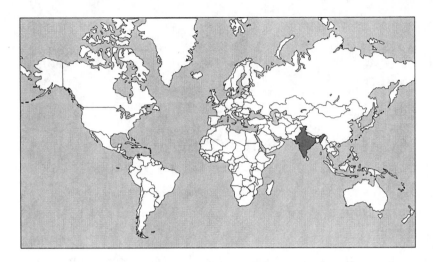

After India's agriculture minister Sharad Pawar was slapped by a young Sikh [a religious minority in India] man at a function in New Delhi, to record his protest against corruption in high places, social media sites went viral with musical spoofs and caricatured images of the incident.

Why This Rage?

It helped the spoofing artists that the assault on the minister, in November 2011, roughly coincided with the bursting on media channels of a chart-busting song, 'Why This Kolaveri Di?' (roughly meaning 'Why this rage?' in Tamil language).

Almost instantly, news channel footage of the slapping incident, set to the tune of the peppy chart buster and with added effects to enhance the resounding slap, became a widely circulated status update on Facebook, the popular social networking site.

The spoof circulated further after someone posted the link on the Facebook wall of 'India Against Corruption', the organization demanding enactment of a strong anti-graft ombudsman law through a movement led by the Gandhian leader Anna Hazare.

Most Popular Online Activity Among Internet Users in India

Online Activity	% Internet Users Undertaking
E-mailing	94%
Downloading Music	72%
Instant Messaging/Chatting	56%
Job Search	56%
PC to Mobile SMS	55%
Social Networking	54%
Info Search Engine	52%
Watch Videos	50%
Screensavers/Wallpapers	50%
Online Communities	50%

Source: India Online Landscape Report 2010.

TAKEN FROM: "India Online Landscape 2010—Internet Usage Statistics for India," *India Microfinance,* July 18, 2010. http://indiamicrofinance.com.

Following this demonstration of social media power, the Indian government announced plans to formulate a framework to regulate "blasphemous and disparaging" contents posted on social networking platforms like Facebook, Google, Microsoft and Yahoo.

India's telecom minister Kapil Sibal asked representatives of major Internet firms to come up with a solution to prevent the posting of material that may hurt religious sentiments. But they remained noncommittal, forcing the government to begin taking steps to formulate a regulatory mechanism.

The judiciary stepped in after a lawsuit filed in the Delhi High Court by a Hindi-Urdu magazine editor demanded that laws banning the sale of obscene books and objects be made applicable to Internet companies.

The judge hearing the case warned that offending Internet sites could be blocked, as in China, if they failed to come up with a way to avoid publishing religiously "offensive and objectionable" content. "Like China, we will block all such websites," Justice Suresh Kait was quoted as saying.

With social media platforms fast turning into a breeding ground for ideas that propel civil society movements, free speech advocates say the move by the Indian government to censor postings is aimed at gagging public opinion under the guise of safeguarding religious sentiments.

"Any such control is based on fear and insecurity. Rising discontent is being taken seriously by the government, so there is an agenda behind the crackdown on the Internet firms," says Gaurav Bakshi, a Delhi-based citizen journalist active in Anna Hazare's anticorruption movement.

"The government is looking out for potential threats to its power, and now that media is covering such issues as corruption we feel concerned," Bakshi told IPS [Inter Press Service].

Vinay Rai, the magazine editor who had filed the criminal lawsuit against the Internet companies, says Internet firms can easily develop mechanisms to block offensive content.

Free speech advocates say the move by the Indian government to censor postings is aimed at gagging public opinion under the guise of safeguarding religious sentiments.

"If they can do business here in India and earn so much, why cannot they also take responsibility and spend something on building a mechanism to block disparaging information?" Rai asked, speaking with IPS.

"We are enjoying freedom of speech, but it does not mean you can hurt religious sentiments of people, or do something that the freedom we enjoy is taken away from us," says Rai.

India Can Be Like China

Media activists already see the government moves as a ploy to curb free speech, especially on the raging issue of corruption.

"It is a myth that the Indian government cannot be like China," says Bakshi, who feels that a move by the government to restrict the number of SMS (short message service over mobile phones) that can be sent in a day was a response to Anna Hazare's anticorruption movement.

Jillian C. York, director of International Freedom of Expression at the Electronic Frontier Foundation in San Francisco, in a column on Indian censorship attempts published on Jan. 20 in Al Jazeera [a Middle Eastern news network], wrote that "unlike books and paintings, online expression cannot easily be hidden from view.

"Try as it might, the Indian government has not managed to succeed in limiting speech it finds distasteful; the offending content, even when blocked, remains accessible to savvy Internet users through use of simple proxies," she wrote.

"You are asking to not just censor the web in India, you are asking to censor the entire World Wide Web."

According to York, censorship of social media has the potential to push India's Internet users over the edge, like the street protestors in Tunisia [where the government was overthrown in 2011].

Blogger and independent journalist Divyanshu Dutta Roy believes that "the independence of the web is what truly makes it wonderful.

"When it comes to offending religious sentiments, I think it will only offend someone if they are looking to be offended," Roy said. "The Internet is not the property of some sensitive religious faction; if they don't like what is being published online, they can simply avoid such web pages.

"A search engine works by letting loose little robot programmes on the Internet called crawlers that index content on websites," said Roy, an expert on technology issues. "I think we are still quite far from the day when these robots can be trained enough to judge what is religiously offensive."

While the government's face-off with the Internet giants rages, a top official from Google said that considering the volume of data posted online daily, it is practically impossible to prescreen it.

Senior vice-president and chief business officer of Google Nikesh Arora told an Indian TV channel at the World Economic Forum in Davos late January [2012] that they are "still open to requests for taking down offensive content once it has been reported by the government or anybody else."

"I think what we are trying to explain is the enormity of what is being asked. You are asking to not just censor the web in India, you are asking to censor the entire World Wide Web. The web has no borders," Arora said.

Cuba's Young People Have Little Access to Social Media

Franco Ordoñez

Franco Ordoñez is a regional correspondent for McClatchy newspapers. In the following viewpoint, he reports that hardly any Cubans have access to the Internet. Ordoñez says that the Cuban government is worried about dissidents using social media and the Internet to protest against the regime. To prevent this, Ordoñez maintains, the government has severely restricted web access. Ordoñez says that some Cubans still manage to post online, but it is very difficult. Though there is a great demand for online access among young people, Ordoñez says that only those in power really have the ability to get online in Cuba.

As you read, consider the following questions:

1. What is the Internet penetration rate in Cuba, and how does Ordoñez say that compares to other nations in the Western Hemisphere?
2. Who is Yoani Sánchez, and how does she communicate with her followers, according to Ordoñez?
3. According to the viewpoint, who is Alan Gross?

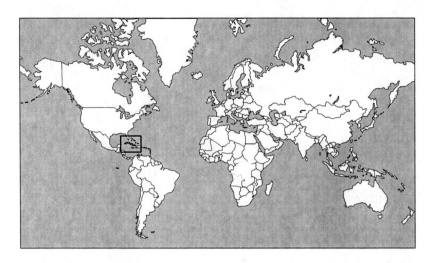

The 24-year-old volunteer shows off the seven computers sitting on wooden desks under a painting of Saint Juan Bosco in a small, 6-by-10-foot cement room at the back of the church.

"We're Ready"

Adalberto Malagon has taken several classes here. He learned how to write book reports on Word and crop photos using Photoshop. But what he really wants to learn is how to surf the web.

Like many young Cubans, Rojas is frustrated that he can't access Facebook and Google like his peers around the world.

"We're ready," he said. "We have so much culture and education in Cuba. There are many Third World countries with much less culture and education than Cuba that have had the Internet for many years."

That may not come for years. Cuba, with its authoritarian Communist government in control of the web, has the lowest Internet-penetration rate in the Western Hemisphere, with just 16 percent of its population online. Even earthquake ravaged Haiti, the hemisphere's poorest country, has a higher percentage of its people on the Internet.

In Cuba, only government officials and foreigners can set up the Internet in their homes, and the vast majority of Cubans can't afford the fees charged at tourist hotels, where an hour of Internet equals about a quarter of the average Cuban's monthly salary.

"Think about it," said David Gonzalez, 20, who sometimes sneaks onto the Internet at the hotel where his mother works. "For $5 an hour, it's not worth it."

Since taking over the presidency from his ailing brother Fidel, Raúl Castro has moved to liberalize the country's economy. He's slowly introducing modern technology. In 2008, islanders first received the right to have private cell phones.

But the government has been more cautious with the World Wide Web. An undersea fiber-optic cable now connecting Cuba and Venezuela will increase the country's bandwidth, but service has yet to begin.

The Cuban government is concerned about the online potential for dissent and social mobilization, according to experts such as William LeoGrande, a Latin America specialist and dean of the American University School of Public Affairs in Washington.

The government feels confident that it has control of the traditional dissident community, LeoGrande said, but it's less familiar with the techniques of a new crop of younger dissidents who've been inspired by the revolutionaries who used social media to start antigovernment movements across North Africa and the Middle East.

Arrested for Carrying Satellite Phones

The most famous Cuban blogger using social media to foment dissent is Yoani Sánchez, who publishes *Generation Y*, which is translated into 16 languages. She sends out regular tweets about activism and her life on the island using text messaging from her cell phone. She has nearly 250,000 Twitter followers. She posts regularly each day.

"It's possible that I don't get there, that I don't have enough health or life, please tell the youth of the future that their irreverence is welcome," she recently wrote on Twitter.

Opponents call her a fraud and an agent in the United States' political and economic war against Cuba.

The greatest challenge bloggers like Sánchez face isn't censorship, but getting online. Despite the restrictions, she and other bloggers are finding new ways to broadcast their reporting, by saving posts onto flash drives and sharing them with friends with access to the Internet.

In 2007, Ramiro Valdés, then the interior minister, called the Internet "one of the mechanisms of global extermination," but he added that it was necessary for continued economic development.

"This concern is exactly why Alan Gross is sitting in prison," LeoGrande said.

"It's possible that I don't get there, that I don't have enough health or life, please tell the youth of the future that their irreverence is welcome."

Gross, an American from suburban Washington, was arrested and accused of being a spy two years ago for bringing satellite phones, laptops and Blackberry cell phones onto the island. Gross worked under the umbrella of a pro-democracy project of the State Department's U.S. Agency for International Development. He said he was bringing the equipment to the island's Jewish community, but he was accused of trying to subvert the government.

The island does have a limited intranet service that is more widely available. Cubans can surf local sites and open e-mail accounts.

Yaremis Guerra, 18, takes classes twice a week at the Youth Computer Club near her home outside Havana, where she looks up music sites and exchanges e-mails with cousins in Texas.

If you asked every young person, . . . they'd tell you their first or second desire is to be able to have more access to the web.

"I get lost in that world," Guerra said.

Jakeline Diaz, 25, has access to e-mail through work at a local hospital near Pinar del Río. But she really longs to get on Facebook. A colleague recently returned from a medical mission in Angola, where she had access to the web and created a Facebook page.

"She has a lot of friends," Diaz said. "She puts up photos. I'd love to have friends from around the world."

On a recent afternoon, Gonzalez was walking with two friends through Old Havana to watch a televised soccer match that he'd learned about on the Internet at his mother's hotel. Since traveling outside the country isn't an option, the Internet is the best way to learn about the outside world, he said. If you asked every young person, he said, they'd tell you their first or second desire is to be able to have more access to the web.

"No one has the Internet," he said. "Not the young people. Not the old people. Really the only people who have the Internet are the people with power."

Periodical and Internet Sources Bibliography

The following articles have been selected to supplement the diverse views presented in this chapter.

BBC News	"India Minister Sibal Says No Censorship of Social Media," February 14, 2012. www.bbc.co.uk.
Andrew Colley	"Every Click You Make, Facebook Tracker Will Be Watching You," *Australian*, September 24, 2011.
Martin Kettle	"To Argue for Controls over the Internet May Not Be Cool, but It's Right," *Guardian*, May 26, 2011.
Louisa Lim	"Two Crises Highlight China's Social Media Struggles," NPR, April 30, 2012. www.npr.org.
Meagan Lunn	"Post-Privacy Era," *Korea IT Times*, February 20, 2012.
Nancy Messieh	"During Elections, Myanmar Journalists Use Social Media to Bypass Government Censorship," The Next Web, April 1, 2012. http://thenextweb.com.
Jason Mick	"Britain Blames Social Media for Class Riots, Looks to Censorship," *DailyTech*, August 12, 2011. www.dailytech.com.
Andres Monroy-Hernandez	"Mexico Murders Show How Internet Empowers, Threatens," CNN, September 16, 2011. www.cnn.com.
Alex Pearlman	"The World's 7 Worst Internet Censorship Offenders," GlobalPost, April 4, 2012. www.globalpost.com.
Spiegel Online	"Facebook Agrees to Voluntary Privacy Code," September 8, 2011. www.spiegel.de.

For Further Discussion

Chapter 1

1. Based on the viewpoints by Jon Russell and Sarah Mishkin, what characteristics do the Philippines and Indonesia have in common that has led social networking to be so popular in those countries? Explain.

2. Do you think social media will continue to grow over the next ten years, or will its growth stall? Provide evidence from the viewpoints in this chapter to defend your opinion.

Chapter 2

1. How do you use social networking? Are any of your uses (for business, to connect with people with similar interests or problems, to follow breaking news) similar to those discussed in this chapter? Provide examples.

Chapter 3

1. The *Economist* is not enthusiastic about the possibility of social networking as a force for democratization. What evidence in this chapter supports the *Economist*'s opinion? What evidence contradicts it?

2. Ethan Zuckerman argues that social media played a role in the revolution in Tunisia but was not solely responsible for the uprising. Do you agree or disagree with Zuckerman's opinion? How do you think social media can help in democratizing other authoritarian regimes around the world? Use examples from the text to support your reasoning.

Chapter 4

1. Based on the viewpoints in this chapter, do you think users overall benefit or are hurt when government intervenes in the regulation of social media? Use specific examples from the chapter to support your opinion.

2. Based on the viewpoints in this chapter, what benefits might there be to using a false name or an alias online? What might be the disadvantages of allowing people to adopt aliases? Explain your answers using examples from this chapter to support your position.

Organizations to Contact

The editors have compiled the following list of organizations concerned with the issues debated in this book. The descriptions are derived from materials provided by the organizations. All have publications or information available for interested readers. The list was compiled on the date of publication of the present volume; the information provided here may change. Be aware that many organizations take several weeks or longer to respond to inquiries, so allow as much time as possible.

American Library Association (ALA)
50 E. Huron Street, Chicago, IL 60611
(800) 545-2433
website: www.ala.org

The American Library Association (ALA) is the oldest and largest library association in the world, with more than sixty-five thousand members. Its mission is to promote the highest quality library and information services, as well as provide public access to information. ALA offers professional services and publications to members and nonmembers. The association supports the use of social networking sites in libraries and classrooms as a part of economic, cultural, and civic life.

Amnesty International
5 Penn Plaza, New York, NY 10001
(212) 807-8400 • fax: (212) 627-1451
e-mail: aimember@aiusa.org
website: www.amnestyusa.org

Amnesty International is a worldwide movement of people who campaign for internationally recognized human rights. Its vision is of a world in which every person enjoys all of the human rights enshrined in the Universal Declaration of Human Rights and other international human rights standards.

Each year, Amnesty International publishes a report on its work and its concerns throughout the world. Its website includes numerous posts that discuss social networking in the context of human rights, such as "Don't Fear the Tweets, Fear the Tweeters" and "Tear Gas Fired and Websites Blocked as Belarus Protesters Are Targeted."

Association of Internet Marketing and Sales Canada (AIMS)
e-mail: admin@aimscanada.com
website: www.aimscanada.com

The Association of Internet Marketing and Sales Canada (AIMS) is a Canadian association for businesspeople looking to use the Internet to expand their businesses and reach new customers. Its members include interactive marketers, salespeople, executives, developers, designers, consultants, business owners, and many others. AIMS delivers education, networking, and discussion through events and online community-building initiatives. Its website includes news, a blog, and information about AIMS events.

Center for Democracy & Technology (CDT)
1634 I Street NW, #1100, Washington, DC   20006
(202) 637-9800
website: www.cdt.org

The Center for Democracy & Technology (CDT) aims to develop public policy solutions that advance constitutional civil liberties and democratic values in new computer and communications media. Pursuing its mission through policy research, public education, and coalition building, the center works to increase citizens' privacy and the public's control over the use of personal information held by government and other institutions. Its publications include issue briefs, policy papers, and blog posts.

Electronic Frontier Foundation (EFF)
454 Shotwell Street, San Francisco, CA   94110-1914
(415) 436-9333 • fax: (415) 436-9993

e-mail: information@eff.org
website: www.eff.org

The Electronic Frontier Foundation (EFF) is an organization of students and other individuals that aims to promote a better understanding of telecommunications issues. It fosters awareness of civil liberties issues arising from advancements in computer-based communications and supports litigation to preserve, protect, and extend First Amendment rights in computing and telecommunications technologies. EFF's publications include the electronic newsletter *EFFector* as well as online bulletins and publications, including "Did Twitter, Facebook Really Build a Revolution?" and "Early Lessons from the Tunisian Revolution."

Federal Trade Commission (FTC)

600 Pennsylvania Avenue NW, Washington, DC 20580
(202) 326-2222
website: www.ftc.gov

The Federal Trade Commission (FTC) is the federal agency that regulates commerce, economic activity, consumer protection, and competition. Its website offers information on online privacy and security issues such as identity theft, Internet fraud, and protecting kids online. It maintains OnGuard Online.gov, which provides information about online scams, viruses, and other Internet security and privacy issues.

Global Internet Freedom Consortium

e-mail: contact@internetfreedom.org
website: www.internetfreedom.org

The Global Internet Freedom Consortium is a group of organizations that develop and deploy anticensorship technologies for use by Internet users in countries whose governments restrict web-based information access. It focuses especially on Internet freedom in China. Its website includes information about its activities, white papers, and research reports such as "Battle for Freedom in Chinese Cyberspace" and "Report on Google.cn's Self Censorship."

Human Rights Watch

350 Fifth Avenue, 34th floor, New York, NY 10118-3299
(212) 290-4700 • fax: (212) 736-1300
e-mail: hrwnyc@hrw.org
website: www.hrw.org

Founded in 1978, Human Rights Watch is a nongovernmental organization that conducts systematic investigations of human rights abuses in countries around the world. It publishes many books and reports on specific countries and issues, as well as annual reports and other articles. Its website includes numerous discussions of human rights and Internet issues, including "Jordan: A Move to Censor Online Expression" and "Bahrain: Rights Activist Jailed for 'Insulting' Tweets."

Internet Services Providers' Association, United Kingdom (ISPA UK)

1 Castle Lane, London SW1E 6DR
020 3397 3304 • fax: 0871 594 0298
e-mail: admin@ispa.org.uk
website: www.ispa.org.uk

The Internet Services Providers' Association (ISPA UK) is the United Kingdom's trade association for Internet service providers. Its mission is to provide essential support for Internet services and promote collaboration between its members and the wider Internet community. It advocates before government bodies on behalf of the Internet industry and users. It publishes *Political Monitor*, a weekly newsletter for members that focuses on political issues affecting the Internet industry. Its website also includes press releases and information about events and policies.

Internet Society (ISOC)

1775 Wiehle Avenue, Suite 201, Reston, VA 20190-5108
(703) 439-2120
e-mail: isoc@isoc.org
website: www.isoc.org

The Internet Society (ISOC)—a group of technologists, developers, educators, researchers, government representatives, and businesspeople—supports the development and dissemination of standards for the Internet. It works to ensure global cooperation and coordination for the Internet and related Internetworking technologies and applications. ISOC publishes the *IETF Journal*, a newsletter, and annual reports.

Bibliography of Books

Lori Andrews   *I Know Who You Are and I Saw What You Did: Social Networks and the Death of Privacy.* New York: Free Press, 2012.

Denis G. Campbell   *Egypt Unshackled: Using Social Media to @#;) the System.* Carmarthenshire, Wales: Cambria Books, 2011.

Ken Coates and Carin Holroyd   *Japan and the Internet Revolution.* New York: Palgrave Macmillan, 2003.

Claire Díaz-Ortiz   *Twitter for Good: Change the World One Tweet at a Time.* San Francisco, CA: Jossey-Bass, 2011.

Robin L. Ersing and Kathleen A. Kost, eds.   *Surviving Disaster: The Role of Social Networks.* Chicago, IL: Lyceum Books, 2012.

Robert Fine, ed.   *The Big Book of Social Media: Case Studies, Stories, Perspectives.* Tulsa, OK: Yorkshire Publishing, 2010.

David Kurt Herold and Peter Marolt, eds.   *Online Society in China: Creating, Celebrating, and Instrumentalising the Online Carnival.* New York: Routledge, 2011.

David T. Hill and Krishna Sen   *The Internet in Indonesia's New Democracy.* New York: RoutledgeCurzon, 2005.

Gregory L. Jantz   *Hooked: The Pitfalls of Media, Technology and Social Networking.* Lake Mary, FL: Charisma House, 2012.

Andrew Keen — *Digital Vertigo: How Today's Online Social Revolution Is Dividing, Diminishing, and Disorienting Us.* New York: St. Martin's Press, 2012.

Rebecca MacKinnon — *Consent of the Networked: The Worldwide Struggle for Internet Freedom.* New York: Basic Books, 2012.

Deborah Micek and Warren Whitlock — *Twitter Revolution: How Social Media and Mobile Marketing Is Changing the Way We Do Business & Market Online.* Las Vegas, NV: Xeno Press, 2008.

Evgeny Morozov — *The Net Delusion: The Dark Side of Internet Freedom.* New York: PublicAffairs, 2011.

Helen Nissenbaum — *Privacy in Context: Technology, Policy, and the Integrity of the Social Life.* Stanford, CA: Stanford University Press, 2010.

John H. Parmelee and Shannon L. Bichard — *Politics and the Twitter Revolution: How Tweets Influence the Relationship Between Political Leaders and the Public.* Lanham, MD: Lexington Books, 2012.

Erik Qualman — *Socialnomics: How Social Media Transforms the Way We Live and Do Business.* Hoboken, NJ: Wiley, 2011.

Russell Southwood — *Less Walk, More Talk: How Celtel and the Mobile Phone Changed Africa.* Hoboken, NJ: Wiley, 2009.

Zixue Tai

The Internet in China: Cyberspace and Civil Society. New York: Routledge, 2006.

Tim Wu

The Master Switch: The Rise and Fall of Information Empires. New York: Vintage Books, 2011.

Index

Geographic headings and page numbers in **boldface** refer to viewpoints about that country or region.

K

Kagan, Robert, 106
Kidnapping, 141
Klimburg, Alexander, 135
Knight Center for Journalism in the Americas, 140
Kobe, Japan Earthquake (1995), 37
Korff, Douwe, 130
Kulow, Tina, 129

L

Languages
    Facebook, African versioning, 34
    Wikipedia inclusion, 12, 13–14
Laptop computers. *See* Personal computers
Latin America, 19
    See also specific Latin American countries
Law360.com, 46
Lee Kuan Yew, 96–97
LeoGrande, William, 151, 152
"Like" button (Facebook), 125, 127–130
Lindsay, David, 117–124
LinkedIn, 47
    Asia market share, 20–21
    journalism use, 54, 56
    Philippines usage rates, 19
    veterans' social networking, 61
Litvinenko, Alexander, 106
Lloyd, John, 102–114
Logan, Samuel, 137–142
Longevity, digital information, 119
Lonkila, Markku, 109
Lucas, Edward, 106

M

Maicih (Indonesian company), 27
Malagon, Adalberto, 150
Malaysia
    population using Facebook, 18, 26
    social networking use, 17, 21
Marketing
    consumer attitudes, cultural differences, 25
    Facebook, 46, 121
    Indonesia as test market, 22, 23, 24, 25
    interactive, 25, 27–28, 31
    research firms, 23, 25
    testimony strategy, 27
Media, traditional. *See* State-controlled media; Traditional media vs. Web 2.0
Media blackouts, 140
Medvedev, Dmitry, 110
Meeker, Mary, 30–31
Memes and spoofs, 143, 144
Mental health-related uses of social networking, 59–66
Mexico, 137–142
    criminal gangs police social media, 137–142
    earthquakes and warning systems, 70
    Facebook use, 44, 47
Mexico City, Mexico, 70
Microblogging
    China, 134
    journalism use, 53, 54, 55, 56
    sites, 20–21
    See also Twitter
Middle class, India, 26
Mig33 (social network), 24
Military veterans' use of social networking, 59–66
Minamisoma, Japan, 38

CPSIA information can be obtained
at www.ICGtesting.com
Printed in the USA
FFOW030702280213